COLD CASE

THE ASSASSINATION OF
PAT GARRETT
INVESTIGATING
HISTORY'S MYSTERIES

W. C. JAMESON

TWODOT®

Guilford, Connecticut
Helena, Montana

A · TWODOT® · BOOK

An imprint of The Rowman & Littlefield Publishing Group, Inc.
4501 Forbes Blvd., Ste. 200
Lanham, MD 20706
A registered trademark of The Rowman & Littlefield Publishing Group, Inc.

Distributed by NATIONAL BOOK NETWORK

British Library Cataloguing in Publication Information available

Library of Congress Cataloging-in-Publication Data

Names: Jameson, W. C., 1942– author.
Title: Cold case: the assassination of Pat Garrett : investigating History's mysteries / W.C. Jameson.
Description: Guilford, Connecticut : TwoDot, [2020] | Includes bibliographical references and index. | Summary: "WC Jameson takes on the myths and discovers what really happened in the Old West by consulting private investigators, using modern forensic techniques, and examining the original evidence."— Provided by publisher.
Identifiers: LCCN 2020005444 (print) | LCCN 2020005445 (ebook) | ISBN 9781493045884 (hardback) | ISBN 9781493045891 (epub)
Subjects: LCSH: Garrett, Pat F. (Pat Floyd), 1850-1908. | Sheriffs—New Mexico—Lincoln County—Biography. | Frontier and pioneer life—Southwest, New. | Garrett, Pat F. (Pat Floyd), 1850-1908—Death and burial. | Lincoln County (N.M.)—Biography. | Southwest, New—Biography.
Classification: LCC F801.G3 J358 2020 (print) | LCC F801.G3 (ebook) | DDC 978.9/6404092 [B]—dc23
LC record available at https://lccn.loc.gov/2020005444
LC ebook record available at https://lccn.loc.gov/2020005445

CONTENTS

PART III: THE ROAD TO ASSASSINATION

PART IV: AFTERMATH

PROLOGUE

Pat Garrett, the once lauded lawman who claimed to have slain the outlaw Billy the Kid, stepped down from the buckboard and unbuttoned the fly on his pants. As he urinated onto the desert sand, he clutched a shotgun in his off hand. The driver of the buggy was standing next to the team of horses, his hands clenching the reins. A man on horseback watched Garrett closely from near the rear of the vehicle. A second later a rifle shot boomed from the arroyo one hundred yards away. A bullet smacked into the back of Garrett's head, passed through his brain, and exited above the left eye. The tall man spun around and fell backward, his head pointed south toward the wagon. He was likely dead. As if to make certain, however, another shot rang out and a second bullet speared into Garrett's stomach at a low angle, passed through his innards, and lodged near the left shoulder.

The driver of the buggy climbed aboard and set off toward Las Cruces, a few miles to the southwest. The man on horseback followed. On arriving in the town, the man on horseback walked into the sheriff's office and confessed to killing Garrett. Legal procedures followed, the man was acquitted, and a celebration followed. There was joy in southern New Mexico; Pat Garrett was dead and those responsible were free.

And then the whisperings began. According to many, the man who confessed to the murder was incapable of such a deed and was known to be inept with firearms, rarely carrying one. A number of suspects entered the conversations, some considered, others dismissed. The "killer," a man who emerged from obscurity and retreated to same, was never mentioned.

INTRODUCTION

THE ASSASSINATION OF THE FAMOUS LAWMAN PAT GARRETT has remained one of the most enduring and perplexing mysteries in the history of the Old West. Controversy has swirled and arguments have raged about the identity of the man who pulled the trigger, as well as the reasons behind the murder, but specific and logical determinations and deductions have remained elusive. The details of the plot that led to the killing, as well as the identity of the participants, have long been debated, and for over a century the murder has been relegated to the status of a cold case, one with nothing resembling a satisfying conclusion.

There are a handful of compelling reasons why the assassination of Pat Garrett has remained a cold case for so many decades; they have to do with the type of individual pursuing the mystery and the manner in which the research is conducted. Western outlaw and lawman research is not densely populated by skilled and credentialed examiners. To state such is not to impugn the motive or integrity of anyone, but merely to underscore a truth that has an impact on results. For the most part, outlaw and lawman research attracts enthusiasts, hobbyists, and those interested in period personalities and events. Many are attracted to the exciting lives and times of Old West characters as a result of film and novels. I have visited with dozens of such men (they always seem to be men, not women) at conventions and conferences where they dress up in real or imagined Old West garb, attend lectures

Pat Garrett, 1890
RICHARD KOLB

and panels, and mingle. Good folks, all of them, and while they stumble from time to time onto some pertinent findings, they are not professionals.

Rarely does outlaw and lawman research attract experienced and credentialed researchers. Many such trained and capable folk are sometimes found associated with colleges and universities, men and a few women with education and experience in proper research technique, hypothesis and null hypothesis formulation, and schooling in the development and carrying out of well-designed inquiry and investigation.

Unfortunately, most colleges and universities do not view western outlaw and lawman research as important enough to support. Research programs and funding are rarely oriented toward such topics.

As a result, the studies conducted by the enthusiasts often lack appropriate and acceptable technique. An extensive examination of such research reveals that it consists mostly of looking up information published by others and copying, with little to no original investigation and interpretation. Thus, while there is an abundance of material on such topics, very little of it is original. In the case of the assassination of Pat Garrett, it was time to not only apply proper and professional research technique, but to inflict an authoritative investigation into the matter. This approach involves treating a killing not so much as an historical event but as a crime scene. The investigator looks for "tells."

A *tell* is a cop term for a sign, always present, that points to the truth. In history, one often encounters tells. A tell can be a witness testimony or a sentence or paragraph that serves to lead one away from the truth, sometimes intentionally, sometimes accidentally. The history of Pat Garrett is filled with tells.

The professional investigator deconstructs an event into its component parts, establishes validity, veracity, and provenance, examines, and then, with all of the elements thoroughly established and analyzed, reconstructs the event. In many cases, what the investigator ends up with is a scenario completely different from what he/she started out with.

In the following pages, Pat Garrett's role in the fierce and bloody days of south-central and southeastern New Mexico during the late 1880s and early 1900s is recounted and the reasons for the then growing animosity and hatred for the former lawman cataloged. As a result of a number of confluent circumstances, it was eventually decided by a select cadre of influential citizens that Garrett had to be eliminated. A plot to do so was hatched, and the participants included prominent ranchers, lawmen, and a highly regarded politician. As a result of new information that has been uncovered, along with a never before undertaken analysis of the crime scene, the plan to eliminate Garrett, as well as the logistics of the killing, are detailed as never before, including the type and caliber of the weapon used.

Furthermore, the assassin of one of the most famous lawmen in the history of the United States is identified with supporting evidence appended.

PART I
PAT GARRETT: MYTH VS. REALITY

CHAPTER 1
WHO WAS PAT GARRETT?

Ask anyone who Pat Garrett was and nearly all will reply that he was the man who killed the outlaw, Billy the Kid. They "know" this because it is what they have always heard; it is what they have seen in movies and on television dozens of times. This is Garrett's brand, this image of the relentless and fearless lawman who pursued, caught up with, and slew, according to him, newspaper accounts, and dime novels, the most notorious outlaw at the time in the American West.

This image has been fortified over the years as a result of film. In the numerous movies that have been produced about Billy the Kid, Sheriff Pat Garrett has invariably been portrayed by actors who were forceful men with a strong presence, including James Coburn, William Petersen, John Dehner, Frank Wilcox, Wallace Beery, James Griffith, Patrick Wayne, Thomas Mitchell, and Glenn Corbett.

Pat Garrett is revered by many. To some, he is the quintessential lawman, a hero who, they are convinced, fought for justice and prevailed. To this day, members of the Lincoln County, New Mexico, sheriff's department wear shoulder patches with an image of Pat Garrett.

Much of what has been written about Pat Garrett is more fiction than truth, a fiction that generated myth and lore regarding the lawman. Garrett himself was in large part responsible for creating this myth, one that he spent most of his life trying to live up to, or retreating into. The myth has been capitalized on and perpetuated. The Pat Garrett character that has appeared in films, in novels, and that has been written about in historical treatments is the imaginary Pat Garrett. The reality is considerably different.

Pat Garrett was the lawman who *claimed* to have shot and killed Billy the Kid. As a result of contemporary investigation, forensic studies, the discovery of lost and overlooked evidence, and a deep and intense parsing and resultant analysis of Garrett's book *The Authentic Life of Billy the Kid* and subsequent publications, a completely different picture of Pat Garrett emerges.

Pat Garrett was a complicated man, a man of solid potential, but one who never achieved a full measure of success. He was, more often than not, governed by his ego rather than logic or common sense. Some insist he was a brave man who faced danger on a regular basis in his role as a lawman. Others point to situations and events in his history that they claim provide the basis for identifying him as a coward. He was, to all appearances, a family man, siring eight children and doting on all of them. At the same time, he consorted openly with prostitutes and had mistresses. He was elected and appointed to uphold the law, but often abused his position and was himself guilty of lawlessness. Some have argued that Garrett was more of an outlaw than Billy the Kid.

Pat Garrett proved himself to be a liar, perhaps a pathological one. This view has been substantiated over and over. He lied and/ or deceived many about a number of things, most of which will be described in the pages of this book. His biggest lie, relating to the deed for which he was granted mythical status, was that he shot and killed Billy the Kid.

Garrett was also a debtor. Had he not been a famous lawman and a well-known, though unsuccessful, rancher, Garrett might well have been jailed for his failure to pay his debts. He owed money to several prominent politicians, businessmen, and others throughout New Mexico, clear up to and including the governor. When Garrett died, a neighboring rancher to whom he owed money took possession of his ranch and was forced to evict his widow and children.

Garrett was a drunk. There exist numerous accounts of Garrett being involved in arguments and scuffles as a result of his drunken belligerence. He had been jailed and fined for such senseless activity.

As a result of his diminishing reputation, his debts, his failing ranch, and his inability to recover from his troubles, most of them self-inflicted, Garrett became a desperate man, one who harbored intense hatred for his enemies, many of whom were his creditors. His growing frustrations, his desperation, his recklessness, and his near-destitute position were factors leading to his assassination.

While Garrett was lauded and recognized during his life-time for his presumed accomplishments and contributions, and praised at his funeral that was attended by state dignitaries, the truth is that during the last years of his life Garrett was despised by most. He had few, if any, friends, and little in the way of any promising future. He was only forty-seven years old when he was assassinated.

CHAPTER 2

ORIGINS

He was born Patrick Floyd Jarvis Garrett on June 5, 1850, in Clarendon County, Alabama. Jarvis was his mother's maiden name. His father, John Lumpkin Garrett, came from a farming family and knew little else. The Garrett farm was barely one of subsistence, and the family just got by. The Garrett family was well acquainted with poverty and hard work.

In 1853, John Lumpkin moved the family to Claiborne Parish, Louisiana, in the northwestern part of the state and near the small town of Homer. There, the elder Garrett obtained a large acreage and undertook farming cotton and vegetables on a grander scale. As soon as he was old enough, Pat, along with his seven siblings, was put to work in the fields. While he did what was required of him, he cared little for farming in general and manual labor in particular. Opportunities in Claiborne Parish, however, were few. His education was described as "spotty," but family lore maintains that Pat liked to read and even possessed a small library. This farm was moderately successful and John Lumpkin provided adequately for his family until the outbreak of the Civil War in 1861.

John Lumpkin Garrett was thirty-nine years old at the onset of the war. It was a time when all able-bodied men were expected to serve and defend the perceived honor of the South, but he was in poor health and did not enlist, nor was he particularly sought after. Among the numerous lies Pat Garrett told throughout his life, one was his insistence that his father served in the War Between the States, and that he attained the rank of colonel. This lie was perhaps a foreshadowing of things to come.

The war proved to be disastrous for the Garrett family. The Union army confiscated John Lumpkin Garrett's cotton crop and he soon found himself deep in debt. He never recovered. In 1867, his wife, Elizabeth, died, and he followed her on December 2, 1868. He left debts totaling $30,000. The settlement of the estate fell into the hands of Larkin Randolph, John Lumpkin's son-in-law. At the time of the elder Garrett's death, Randolph operated a tavern and brothel in Shongaloo, Louisiana, near the Arkansas border.

When all was said and done, Pat and his siblings received nothing, with Randolph awarding himself most of the assets. Garrett, eighteen years old, tall, and quick-tempered, threatened to kill Randolph, but was talked out of it by his sister Margaret, Randolph's wife. Angry, Pat loaded what little he owned onto the back of a horse and rode away, never to return to the family fold.

CHAPTER 3
WESTBOUND

FOR THE NEXT SEVEN YEARS AFTER LEAVING LOUISIANA, PAT Garrett's doings and whereabouts are a mystery. A March 1875 article in a Bowie County, Texas, newspaper referred to an incident wherein a man named "Pat Garrity" was arrested for killing a black man. Bowie County is one hundred miles northwest of Homer, Louisiana. The man identified as Garrity escaped from the county jail. According to the article, a posse pursued him for three hundred miles before turning back. Throughout his life, Garrett never referred to this incident, and it has never been formally verified that he was the murderer.

Not long after the Bowie County incident, however, Garrett showed up in Dallas County, Texas, where he found work clearing land. He did not last long at this job, as the tedium of such work did not appeal to him. He soon found himself back in Louisiana where he, along with others, was employed by a rancher to drive a herd of cattle to Dodge City, Kansas. At least one account has Garrett leaving the drive near Dennison, Texas, and continuing westward. Other accounts have him fulfilling his responsibilities and taking the herd on to Dodge City.

Though specific data is lacking, there has long been a tale that Garrett settled in for a time at Sweetwater, Texas. There, according to writer Eve Ball, he married and had a child, and a short time later abandoned his family. Ball, a respected author and researcher, claimed she had evidence of the marriage and knew the name of Garrett's wife. Because of potential embarrassment to certain individuals, according to Ball, she refused to release the specifics. Garrett's descendants have denied the claim.

Sometime during the mid-1870s, Garrett met Willis Skelton Glenn in Tarrant County, Texas. Glenn was a buffalo hunter and hired Garrett as part of a team to hunt, skin, and transport buffalo hides to the nearest shipping point where they were forwarded to locations in the East. There, they were fashioned into coats, rugs, and other items popular with the citizenry at the time. After purchasing supplies and provisions, the team set out for the buffalo range near Fort Griffin, Texas.

During these times, Fort Griffin was not a place for the faint of heart. Save for buffalo hunters, gamblers, outlaws, prostitutes, and a few cowhands and soldiers, the place was generally avoided. The buffalo hunters depended on Fort Griffin for their supplies and recreation. When Glenn's team of hunters and skinners arrived, they loaded up on items they needed such as guns, ammunition, skinning knives, saddles, bridles, harnesses, bacon, beans, flour, molasses, coffee, tobacco, and corn for the horses. After leaving Fort Griffin, the party headed out to the Double Mountains in the southern part of the Panhandle and set up camp.

After several days of successful hunting, Glenn returned to Fort Griffin to have a rifle repaired. Back at the Double Mountains, the weather was cold and rainy and not fit for hunting. Garrett and his companions remained in camp trying to keep a fire going with limited success. The men were depressed and edgy. Garrett insulted a member of the party, a man named Briscoe. A confrontation followed, and Briscoe picked up an axe and came after Garrett, who shot him in the chest, killing him. Worried that he would be charged with murder, Garrett saddled his horse and left camp. Glenn returned to the encampment the next day and learned what had occurred. Between the bad weather and not having any destination in mind, Garrett eventually returned to the camp, and told his side of the story to Glenn. Glenn talked Garrett into riding to Fort Griffin and explaining to the sheriff what had happened. He did so, found that the Fort Griffin lawmen were not at all interested in arresting him, and returned to the camp.

Glenn's team continued harvesting buffalo, but were now forced to deal with raiding Comanches, who were attacking the camps and occasionally killing a hunter. While Garrett and another member of the party were out shooting buffalo, the Comanches raided their hunting camp and destroyed most of the accumulated hides. After selling the salvaged hides, Glenn and Garrett took a train to St. Louis, Missouri, where they drank and gambled away the few profits they had earned. Following this, they returned to Fort Griffin with plans to set out again on a buffalo hunt. By January 1878, however, it was becoming clear to Glenn and other hunters that there were not enough buffalo left on the range to provide a living. In February, Garrett, in the company of Glenn and another man named Nick Buck, decided to travel to New Mexico.

Several years later, Willis Glenn sued the US government for $15,000 for losses incurred during the Indian raids. He claimed that the government was "negligent in maintaining the Indians on the reservation." The claim dragged on for years and finally came to trial in 1899. Pat Garrett was called to testify.

After being sworn in, Garrett stated that Glenn's total losses amounted to no more than $1,000. Stunned at the testimony of his old partner, Glenn was unable to provide any evidence to dispute Garrett's statement. The case remained in the courts for several years and was heard again in 1912, four years after Garrett had been assassinated. Glenn's strategy this time around was to call into question Garrett's integrity and character. Glenn pointed out that Garrett had acquired a reputation as a dishonest and untrustworthy individual. Several prominent members of society were called to the stand to testify and stated under oath that Garrett was dishonest, a drunk, a womanizer, a gambler, an agnostic, a debtor, and that his capacity for truth was lacking. Garrett, who had been in his grave for years, was unable to defend himself, but others came forth and stated that the deceased was "truthful," "brave," "unsullied," and "honorable."

Glenn's persistence, however, finally paid off. After thirteen years of pushing his claim through the courts, he was eventually awarded $4,140. From this amount, he had to pay his lawyer 20 percent.

CHAPTER 4
NEW MEXICO

PAT GARRETT, ALONG WITH WILLIS GLENN AND NICK BUCK, crossed the rolling southeastern plains of New Mexico, eventually arriving at the small town of Fort Sumner. Having little money for a hotel room, the three men set up camp outside of town near the bank of the Pecos River. After pooling the last of their coins, Garrett went into town and purchased a small amount of bacon and flour. While settled in at this location, Garrett noticed a herd of cattle being driven from one pasture to another. Somewhat experienced with livestock, Garrett decided to seek out the owner of the herd and ask to be hired on. The owner was Pete Maxwell, who offered Garrett a job. Glenn and Buck broke camp and continued westward.

Pete Maxwell was the son of Lucien Bonaparte Maxwell. The elder Maxwell moved onto land that had once been owned by the federal government and which for a time served as a prison camp for thousands of Navajo and Apache Indians. As a result of inept administration, the project was abandoned in 1869, the buildings sold to Lucien in 1871. He moved onto the land and established a successful cattle ranch. In 1875, Lucien passed away, and his son Pedro, known as Pete, took over the operation.

On the days he was not working cattle, Garrett hung around the small town of Fort Sumner. It was here that he met the man who would come to be known as Billy the Kid. At the time, the Kid was using the alias William Bonney, and over the next several months operated under other names, including Henry Antrim and Henry McCarty. His real name, it was discovered in the 1940s and verified during the 1990s, was William Henry Roberts. (See *Billy the Kid: Beyond the Grave*, 2005.) A story had made the rounds that in 1879 the Kid, noticing that Garrett's boots were worn out, took up a collection from his friends and bought him a new pair.

During the time of New Mexico's famous Lincoln County War (February 18, 1878–July 19, 1878), Pat Garrett was working as a bartender in Roswell, far from the conflict. Billy the Kid had an active part in the so-called war and began to solidify his reputation as a daring young outlaw. Over the years, the myth and legend of Billy the Kid, as well as that of Pat Garrett, grew and expanded well beyond the truth.

On April 1, the Kid, along with several of his confederates, fired at Lincoln County sheriff William Brady and three of his deputies as they made their way down the main street of Lincoln. Brady and Deputy George Hindman were gunned down. Lawmen undertook pursuit of the Kid. He was eventually captured and charged with the murder of Brady and Hindman. Following a series of adventures and confrontations, the Kid finally surrendered to the new Lincoln County sheriff, George Kimbrell (sometimes seen in the literature as Kimball). Prosecuting attorney William R. Rynerson had the Kid indicted for the murder of Sheriff Brady and Deputy Hindman. The trial venue was moved to the Mesilla courthouse in Doña Ana County. The Kid, who was represented by Albert Jennings Fountain, was found guilty and sentenced to hang on May 13, 1881. (Fountain would reappear later in ongoing New Mexico events and would factor significantly in the life of Pat Garrett.)

The stage was now set for one of the grand dramas in the life of Pat Garrett. Garrett and Billy the Kid were on an inevitable collision course, and as it turned out, the reputations and legends associated with both men were the result of their interactions and confrontations. Each man, oddly, was responsible for creating the legend for the other.

CHAPTER 5

THE NEW SHERIFF

LINCOLN COUNTY SHERIFF GEORGE KIMBRELL HAD AN UNDIS-
tinguished record as a law enforcement officer. While cattle and
horse rustling was near epidemic in the area, Kimbrell remained
hidden away in his office. When those affected by livestock theft
informed Kimbrell where the outlaws and the stolen herds were
encamped, he refused to undertake investigation or pursuit. Both
ranchers and citizens were getting fed up. Influential cattleman
John Chisum wrote a letter to New Mexico governor Lew Wallace decrying the situation in Lincoln County and the inept law
enforcement. In his letter, Chisum recommended Pat Garrett as a
suitable replacement for the reigning sheriff. Garrett, he claimed,
had the capability of organizing effective pursuit and capture of
the rustlers.

Chisum, along with Roswell resident Joseph C. Lee, traveled
to Fort Sumner and approached Garrett about running for the
office of sheriff. Garrett agreed to move to Roswell in time to
qualify for the November 2, 1880, election. He would oppose
Kimbrell in the contest for sheriff.

Both candidates ran on the Democratic ticket. With the
support of Chisum, Garrett won the nomination. Not one to give
up easily, Kimbrell decided to run for the office as an independent. Meanwhile, Chisum managed to enlist support for Garrett

among other ranchers. At the time, there were a significant number of Mexican-American voters. In addition to recently being married to the former Apolinaria Gutierrez, Garrett got along well with the citizens of Mexican descent. By the time the polls closed, Garrett won the election: 320 votes to Kimbrell's 179.

Garrett lost no time in going after the rustlers, and claimed some successes on that front. To add to his responsibilities as the chief law enforcement officer of the county, Garrett had been informed by the US Treasury Department that the passing of counterfeit bills was rampant in Lincoln County. One of those involved with the counterfeiting operation was Billy the Kid, also a known cattle thief. By this time, between the rustling activities and the involvement in the counterfeiting schemes, Pat Garrett's chief responsibility became the pursuit of Billy the Kid. The sheriff did so with renewed enthusiasm, for removing this particular threat to the livestock of Lincoln County would surely elevate his status among voters. Garrett was already pondering the notion of running for higher office. He intended to capture or kill the Kid, for such an achievement, he considered, could generate greater name recognition, an important consideration when running for higher office.

Pursuit of Billy the Kid, along with the gang he ran with, led Garrett on a chase that took his posse and him throughout much of Lincoln County and nearby areas. Dedicated to the task, the determined sheriff eventually succeeded in tracking the outlaws to a remote rock cabin at a location called Stinking Springs. In the dark of night on December 21, Garrett halted the posse about one-half mile from the cabin. Dismounting, they approached the hideout in silence and waited for the dawn. As the members of the posse took positions behind outcrops and trees, Garrett passed the word that their primary mission was to kill Billy the Kid. Once the Kid was dead, he told them, the rest of the gang would likely surrender.

As the first hint of sunrise appeared over the eastern horizon, Garrett and his deputies could hear the sounds of the men in the cabin rousing from their slumber. Presently, one of the outlaws—Charlie Bowdre—stepped through the doorway and approached one of the horses with a feedbag. He was wearing a heavy coat and a sombrero pulled low over his face. Believing the man to be Billy the Kid, Garrett called out for him to raise his hands. At the sound of the voice, Bowdre turned, pulled two revolvers, and fired. His actions were immediately responded to with rifle fire, one bullet striking him in the leg, two in the torso. Garrett realized at that point that it was not the Kid, but his friend Bowdre. Screaming in pain, the wounded outlaw staggered back into the cabin.

Quiet reigned for the next several minutes. One of the gang members, Billy Wilson, called out to Garrett that Bowdre was "killed and wanted to come out." Bowdre was shoved out the door with instructions to kill as many of the lawmen as he could. He stumbled toward Garrett and other posse members, his hands in the air. Garrett caught him as he started to collapse. Bowdre died moments later.

Garrett ordered his men to surround the rock house. Presently, the lawmen heard sounds of digging. Louis Bousman, one of the posse members, said, "Billy and his outfit began trying to dig portholes in that rock building. There was only one north window and one west door. Pat said, 'There is no use for us to lay there all day, we better get away before they do get portholes.'"

Later in the afternoon, the Kid told Garrett that they were ready to surrender. Tom Pickett exited the rock house first, carrying a white cloth in his right hand. He was followed by Billy Wilson and Dave Rudabaugh. The Kid did not come out. The posse members waited for several minutes, and then the Kid announced that he was ready to come out. It was late in the afternoon.

Once the Kid was under guard, Garrett entered the cabin. Inside, he discovered that the Kid had piled up all of the weapons, as well as gun belts in one corner of the structure, and urinated on them. If Garrett wanted them, he had to clean them. The pile of urine-covered weapons and gear was a brilliant tactic employed by the Kid, one that fooled Garrett completely.

One of the reasons Garrett was pursuing the Kid was because he had been assigned to chase down those who were passing counterfeit money. If the Kid and his gang were caught with the fake bills, it would have been in violation of a federal law. The five outlaws were trapped inside a rock house with no chance for escape; the only clear option was to surrender. They did not want to be caught in possession of the counterfeit money. They had a fire going inside the cabin and they could have burned the money, but if they did then they would lose it. There first choice would be to hide it and return for it later. But where?

When Garrett's men heard the sounds of digging, they assumed the outlaws were creating portholes from which they could fire upon the lawmen. History proves this observation to be dead wrong. First, the house was made of rock; they were not going to be able to dig through rock without extreme difficulty. Second, since it was clear the gang was going to have to eventually surrender to the posse, it made no sense that they would go to the great trouble to dig portholes. Third, portholes were never found in the building and are never mentioned again in the historical record. Conclusion: The Kid and his gang were not digging portholes; they were digging a hole in the dirt floor of the rock house in which to bury the counterfeit money. Into the hole they excavated, they placed the counterfeit bills and a Colt .45 revolver.

There is even more evidence for this caching of the counterfeit money. Weeks later when Billy the Kid effected an escape from the law, John F. Meadows suggested to him that he flee to Mexico. The Kid told Meadows that he had no money, that he had "to go back and get a little before I leave." Note that the Kid did not state that he had to go back and *make* some money, or *steal* some money. He said he had to go back and *get* some money. Most likely he was referring to the money he had cached at the rock house.

More evidence: In 1912, Tom Pickett, one of the Kid's gang members who was captured at Stinking Springs, was living in Arizona, an elderly man and surviving on a small pension. Pickett was in need of money and, according to Phillip J. Rasch who interviewed him, "sent Ed Coles to dig up a lot of money which the Kid's gang had buried before their surrender at Stinking Springs. Cole found the spot, but the money was all paper and had rotted away."

There is evidence that the money did not rot away at all, but was retrieved, most likely by the Kid. The gun, rusted and unfit for use as a result of lying in the ground for so long, was left behind. During the summer of 1910, nine-year-old Ralph Camp was digging a hole in the corner of the old rock house at Stinking Springs. Only a few inches below the surface, he found a handgun, a Colt .45 revolver, still loaded. (For more details on Billy the Kid's involvement with the counterfeit money scheme, see *Billy the Kid: Investigating History's Mysteries*, 2018.)

CHAPTER 6

PRISONER

Billy the Kid, along with Dave Rudabaugh, Billy Wilson, and Tom Pickett, were now the prisoners of Pat Garrett and were held in the jail at Las Vegas, New Mexico. The next order of business for the lawman was to have the prisoners delivered to the US marshal at Santa Fe. Garrett decided to take the Kid, Rudabaugh, and Wilson and leave Pickett behind, stating that the only reason he arrested him was because he was with the others, but he was not guilty of anything. As he prepared to have the prisoners transferred, a dispute arose over jurisdictional authority. Only the Kid and Wilson were handed over to him. When Garrett demanded that Rudabaugh be included, he learned that local authorities planned for him to remain in custody as a result of previous crimes, including the killing of a jailer during an earlier escape. Garrett informed the locals that he was a deputy US marshal and as such held a higher claim to Rudabaugh relative to another earlier offense—the robbery of mail sacks during a train holdup. That, stated Garrett, made Rudabaugh a federal prisoner. Garrett prevailed and he escorted his cuffed and chained prisoners to the train station.

On the way to the depot, a crowd began gathering and shouting demands that Rudabaugh be turned over to them. The jailer Rudabaugh killed was a popular man in town and retribution was on the mind of the mob. Garrett secured his prisoners in a private railroad car. Several minutes later as the train got under way, several armed men climbed onto the engine, pointed revolvers at the engineer, and demanded that he pull to a halt. When the train stopped, Garrett, after assigning his deputy to guard the prisoners, stepped out of the car and onto the platform just in time to see Las Vegas deputy sheriff Desiderio Romero, in the company of five men, climbing onto the train. As Romero reached the top step, Garrett stopped him. Romero turned toward the growing crowd and announced that he was going to enter the car and retrieve Rudabaugh. This was greeted with cheers. Garrett responded by pulling his revolver, pointing it at the deputy, and instructing him and his men to leave. With Garrett looming over him and the revolver in his face, Romero did as instructed.

Another deputy US marshal—J. F. Morley—arrived and volunteered to assist Garrett. Garrett asked Morley to go to the nearby Santa Fe Railroad office and request that chief engineer A. F. Robinson furnish a crew to get the train to Santa Fe. Robinson refused to help. The angry Morley stomped out of the office and back to the depot. He climbed into the locomotive, examined all of the levers and switches, and began manipulating them. Moments later, the train was under way. In Santa Fe, the prisoners were handed over to Deputy US Marshal Charles Conklin.

Wielding his revolver, Garrett had managed to thwart the angry crowd and the Las Vegas law enforcement authorities and deliver Billy the Kid to Santa Fe.

While in the jail at Santa Fe, the Kid and Rudabaugh made plans to escape by using kitchen utensils to dig a tunnel. They were reported by a fellow prisoner, their plan thwarted. Several weeks later Rudabaugh was transferred back to the Las Vegas jail where he was to be hanged. This time, he effectively dug his way out of the cell and escaped into Mexico. For his efforts, Billy the Kid was placed in solitary confinement where he was to await his trial date. On March 28, he was transported from Santa Fe to Mesilla, New Mexico, where he was to stand trial for the killing of Sheriff William Brady, Morris Bernstein (an Indian reservation clerk), and a man named Buckshot Roberts. The charges relating to Roberts and Bernstein were dropped because the prosecution perceived a number of weaknesses in each case.

On April 8, the trial got underway and lasted only two days. The defense provided by lawyer Albert Jennings Fountain proved to be unsuccessful, and the Kid was found guilty. On April 15, Judge Warren Bristol read the order that Billy the Kid was to be delivered to the custody of Lincoln County sheriff Pat Garrett and on May 13, 1881, was to be "hanged by the neck until his body be dead."

The trial and sentencing of Billy the Kid represented another chapter in the ongoing saga between the outlaw and Pat Garrett, one that would now gain momentum.

CHAPTER 7

LINCOLN COUNTY JAIL

As plans were being made to deliver Billy the Kid to the Lincoln County jail, Pat Garrett was reveling in the newspaper coverage and editorial praise related to his capture of the noted outlaw. An ego-driven man, Garrett basked in the recognition, the subsequent handshaking and congratulations.

Garrett, always in need of funds, looked forward to collecting the $500 reward offered for the capture of Billy the Kid. He filed a claim with the governor's office in Santa Fe, but received no reply. As it turned out, Governor Lew Wallace was on a book-signing tour of the East. His novel, *Ben-Hur*, was selling briskly, and Wallace was enjoying his own enhanced level of fame.

On learning this, Garrett re-filed his claim for the reward with acting governor W. C. Ritch. Ritch messaged back to Garrett that he had no authority to release such funds. To Garrett's dismay, Ritch also expressed doubts about the legitimacy of the claim. Ritch explained to Garrett that the reward was for the capture and delivery of Billy the Kid to the sheriff of Lincoln County. Since Garrett would not legally assume the office of sheriff until January 1, he was not eligible for the reward, and since he had not delivered the outlaw to the current sheriff, George Kimbrell, he was therefore disqualified from consideration for not complying with the specific conditions.

Newspapers and citizens who were sympathetic to the lawman lobbied Ritch to pay the reward, but the acting governor was not moved to do so. Garrett supporters argued that he was acting sheriff at the time, but their case fell on deaf ears. In the end, citizens raised the $500 from donations and presented the money to Garrett. Garrett invested some of the money in a ranch and went through the rest gambling and drinking.

While Garrett was being lauded for capturing the Southwest's most notorious outlaw, Billy the Kid was being delivered to the Lincoln County jail. He was escorted from Mesilla to Lincoln by no less than seven armed lawmen, not including the sheriff. Shackled and chained, the Kid was placed in a horse-drawn ambulance. Seated next to him was US Marshal Robert Olinger. In the role of guard and escort to Billy the Kid, Olinger was soon to assume another important role in what would become a growing and controversial drama.

Robert Olinger was not well liked, even by other lawmen. He was described as "an obnoxious bully" and had killed men in cold blood by shooting them in the back. During the trip from Mesilla to Lincoln, Olinger, carrying a shotgun, continually tormented and threatened the Kid. On arriving at the Lincoln County courthouse, the Kid was taken to the jail, a northeast room on the second story, and chained to an iron eyebolt in the floor near the fireplace. When Garrett arrived at the courthouse, he dismissed all of the posse members save for Olinger, who was assigned to guard the outlaw while he awaited hanging. Olinger was assisted by Deputy Sheriff J. W. Bell.

Chained and cuffed, the Kid was taunted and bullied by the hateful Olinger, who continued to hurl threats at the defenseless young man. Bell, unlike Olinger, was a quiet, pleasant man and got along well with the Kid. During idle hours Bell and the Kid played checkers or cards. Garrett was nowhere around; he had gone to White Oaks ostensibly to collect taxes. His absence was to prove embarrassing.

At noon on April 28, Olinger, after placing his shotgun in a gun cabinet, escorted some prisoners across the street to the Wortley Hotel for lunch. Bell remained to guard the Kid. Minutes later Bell was dead.

CHAPTER 8
ESCAPE

THE ESCAPE OF BILLY THE KID FROM THE LINCOLN COUNTY JAIL on April 28, 1881, has been written about hundreds of times in books and articles and portrayed in film. It has been repeated so often that most regard it as fact. This long-accepted version of the event went unchallenged for three-quarters of a century. Yet, an authentic, formal, police investigation never took place until August 2004.

In general, this is what we believe occurred after Marshal Olinger departed with prisoners for the dining room at the Wortley Hotel. Billy the Kid was somehow freed from his cuffs and moments later shot and killed Deputy Bell. This done, he went to the gun cabinet and retrieved Olinger's shotgun. On hearing the shot that killed Bell, Olinger rose from his meal at the Wortley Hotel and made his way back across the street to the courthouse to investigate. It is likely that he believed Bell had killed the Kid. As Olinger neared the northeast corner of the courthouse, the Kid stepped up to an open second floor window, pointed Olinger's own shotgun at him, and fired both barrels, killing him instantly. Still shackled at the ankles, the Kid descended to the first floor, had someone bring him a horse, and rode away.

Most of the details related to the Kid's escape—what occurred in the courthouse, how Bell was killed, and the escape—were provided by one person: Pat Garrett. Events that took place outside the courthouse were reported by eyewitnesses. At the time all of this was transpiring, however, Garrett was thirty miles away and not privy to the goings-on. Garrett apologists explain that he relied heavily on an account provided by Gottfried Gauss, who was employed as a caretaker for the courthouse. Gottfried, like Garrett, was not inside the courthouse or the jail and could not have known what had taken place. Garrett's description of Bell's murder, therefore, was concocted out of whole cloth.

In 1955, a book published by the University of New Mexico Press introduced a completely different scenario of what took place on that fateful day inside the courthouse. *Alias Billy the Kid* by C. L. Sonnichsen and William V. Morrison recounted the recollections of a man named William Henry Roberts who had been formally identified in 1948 as the outlaw, Billy the Kid. It is important to note that only two men—the Kid and Deputy Bell—were privy to what actually occurred on the second floor of the courthouse. Bell was dead, and the Kid, in the form of Roberts, returned sixty-eight years later to tell his side of the story.

Garrett's version of the Kid's escape is recounted in the book that bears his name as author, *The Authentic Life of Billy the Kid* (1882). More on this later, but suffice to say that historians agree that little in that publication resembles the truth. Pat Garrett was a man with a large ego and was a known liar. Thus, his word cannot be trusted.

An intensive and ongoing examination of the account and description of what happened on the day of the escape provided by William Henry Roberts, aka Billy the Kid, is something different altogether. Roberts's claim that he was the Kid was dismissed and ridiculed by the cadre of outlaw and lawman enthusiasts who insisted on sticking with the status quo, i.e., Garrett's version of the events. On the other hand, competent investigators, who had learned not to trust anything credited to Garrett, examined in depth every statement made by Roberts that appeared in print. In virtually every instance, Roberts proved to be more credible than the lawman. In the end, Roberts's trustworthiness and veracity far exceeded that of Pat Garrett.

The details of the escape of Billy the Kid from the Lincoln County courthouse have been subjected to intense investigation—deconstruction, analysis, provenance accounting, and reconstruction—and can be found in *Billy the Kid: Beyond the Grave* (2005) and *Billy the Kid: Investigating History's Mysteries* (2018).

Billy the Kid was now on the run. Under sentence to hang for the killing of Sheriff William Brady, as well as the recent killing of two additional lawmen, he was well aware that he would be pursued with renewed vigor. He also knew that Pat Garrett would be leading the pursuit, and as long as he remained in the vicinity of Lincoln and Fort Sumner, confrontation was inevitable.

Garrett, on the other hand, seemed none too eager to encounter the Kid. When he received the news of the Kid's escape and the killing of Olinger and Bell, he was miles away in White Oaks. On returning to Lincoln, he organized several posses and instructed them to search throughout the area for the outlaw. The posses traveled as far east as the Panhandle of Texas, but no sign of Billy the Kid could be found. Rumors spread throughout the area that he had fled to Mexico.

Weeks passed with no sign of the Kid, and citizens were beginning to question Garrett's leadership. His reputation as an effective and efficient lawman began to fade. When New Mexico residents spoke of the Kid now, they talked about his bravery and daring as manifested by his escape from the Lincoln County jail. The Kid, already well known and popular with many of the Mexican citizens, was raised to the status of hero, a clever outlaw who had thwarted the plots and plans of the gringo lawmen.

When area citizens spoke of Garrett now, they said he encountered and captured Billy the Kid as a result of sheer luck, and he was not given much of a chance that he would accomplish it again. In addition, it was clear to many New Mexicans that Garrett was aligned with the territory's political and economic power base, a structure that generally ignored the needs of the Mexicans. Not only was the Kid a favorite of the Mexicans, he was admired by many Anglo owners of small ranches who themselves felt the pressure from elected officials and others who sought to determine how the county was run. Many of these same men detested Garrett and regarded him as a puppet of those in power.

Weeks passed, and Garrett had reported no success in locating or capturing Billy the Kid. Many interpreted this as a lack of concern by the lawman; others openly stated that they believed Garrett was afraid of the Kid, afraid of another confrontation. Garrett heard the talk; his concerns grew and his confidence was shaken. He was aware of the growing disdain for him and his paltry efforts. During the first week of June, Garrett threatened to resign as sheriff unless citizens manifested greater support for him.

Texas Panhandle ranchers who had experienced livestock losses that they attributed to Billy the Kid and his gang took up a collection to assist in funding the search. The effort was led by Texas cattleman Charles Goodnight. Sensing that Garrett might be incapable of locating Billy the Kid on his own, Goodnight enlisted the services of John W. Poe that were paid for by the cattlemen.

John Poe
RICHARD KOLB

Poe had been a deputy sheriff in Wheeler County, Texas, and held a commission as a deputy US marshal. He was highly respected, regarded as a competent, honest, and fair lawman. He was introduced to Garrett in March 1881. Garrett turned the responsibility of locating the Kid and submitting a report over to Poe.

Not long after Poe arrived in New Mexico, Governor Lew Wallace returned from his book tour. On being apprised of the goings-on in Lincoln County involving Billy the Kid, he posted a $500 reward for anyone who captured the Kid and delivered him to any sheriff in New Mexico. Most regarded this offer as a slap in the face of Garrett and what were perceived to be his futile efforts in tracking down the outlaw. Few lawmen manifested any enthusiasm for going after the Kid, preferring instead to believe the tales that he had fled to Mexico.

Known to almost everyone but law enforcement authorities, however, was the fact that Billy the Kid was in Fort Sumner and living on Pete Maxwell's ranch. This choice on the part of the outlaw was to set the stage for a final showdown with Pat Garrett, a confrontation that would forever cement the image of the lawman in the minds of the American populace. As it turned out, it would become an image based on a lie.

CHAPTER 9

THE SHOOTING AT FORT SUMNER

Near midnight on July 14, 1881, Pat Garrett was only minutes away from cementing his legend as a fearless lawman. He, along with deputies John Poe and Thomas McKinney, had arrived at the Maxwell Ranch at Fort Sumner. The lawmen were acting on information recently gleaned by Poe. At first, Garrett was unconvinced that the Kid was hanging out in the area and was all for returning to Lincoln, but Poe dissuaded him.

Approaching the building where Pete Maxwell lived, Garrett ordered Poe and McKinney to remain outside and keep watch while he went inside and spoke with the rancher. Garrett woke Maxwell up and was conversing with him when a young man walked up to Poe and McKinney. Following the exchange of a few words, the newcomer slipped into the building and then into Maxwell's bedroom. Believing the stranger to be Billy the Kid, Garrett shot, his bullet striking the man in the chest and killing him. Garrett claimed he then "threw my body aside and fired again."

Based on a forensic analysis of the shooting (reported in *Billy the Kid: Investigating History's Mysteries*, 2018), Garrett did indeed throw his body aside. Apparently in a panic, Garrett dropped to the floor and scrambled around on his hands and knees, eventually firing his revolver again and striking a bedside table. Regaining his feet, Garrett then dashed outside the building whereupon he met Poe and McKinney. He told them, "That was the Kid that came in there onto me, and I think I have got him." Poe responded by informing Garrett he had shot the wrong man. How prophetic Poe's comments were to become.

Garrett's explanations and descriptions of what occurred in Pete Maxwell's bedroom, along with the reported subsequent events, are replete with contradictions and discrepancies. To further shed doubt on an already suspicious event, there were three inquests performed, in which the written record of one appeared to have been dictated by Garrett himself and it recommended he be given the reward money. Furthermore, this inquest report bore the signatures of men who were not present at the time it was drafted.

In a complete reversal of the tradition of the time, Garrett ordered that the body of the man he shot be interred almost immediately. In the case of an outlaw or outlaws who had been killed, it was standard practice to display the bodies for all to see. It was not uncommon for the lawman in charge to pose with the dead outlaw. Garrett, however, lost no time at all in getting the man he had shot underground, an odd decision. As a politician, Garrett aspired to higher office. Posing with the corpse of what newspapers had described as the most notorious outlaw in the Southwest would have certainly done wonders for his fledgling political career. But the body was posthaste prepared and buried. Even at that point, there were whisperings around Fort Sumner that Garrett had killed the wrong man, and the Kid got away. Over the years, the rumors grew and intensified. While the Anglo population lauded Garrett for his prowess as a lawman, the Mexican population of this part of the state knew that the sheriff was lying. (Details of the investigations and conclusions relative to the shooting, the inquests, and the burial of the man Pat Garrett claimed was the Kid can found in *Billy the Kid: Beyond the Grave* and *Billy the Kid: Investigating History's Mysteries*.)

CHAPTER 10
THE BOOK

A FEW WEEKS FOLLOWING THE SHOOTING OF THE MAN PAT Garrett claimed was Billy the Kid, Charles W. Greene, the editor of the *Santa Fe New Mexican*, approached the lawman and suggested that he write a book about his pursuit and final confrontation with Billy the Kid. Garrett agreed, and Greene informed him he would publish it. Apparently aware that Garrett was not capable of penning the manuscript himself, Greene recommended that he find someone to write it for him. Garrett contacted a friend, Ashmon Upson, and invited him to be involved in the project. Upson was a former newspaperman, real estate salesman, postmaster, and notary public. Like Garrett, Upson had a propensity for alcohol. In addition to drinking, both men loved gambling, horse racing, and loose women.

With Upson's assistance, Garrett pursued the challenge of writing a book. The ultimate product was released with the weighty title *The Authentic Life of Billy, the Kid, the Noted Desperado of the Southwest, Whose Deeds of Daring Have Made His Name a Terror in New Mexico, Arizona, and Northern Mexico.* Though Garrett is listed as the sole author, it has been acknowledged by researchers that most, if not all, of the publication was written by Upson. In an interview that was published in James D. Shinkle's *Reminiscences of Roswell Pioneers*, Upson claimed that he wrote

Ashmon Upson
RICHARD KOLB

every word of the book and was ultimately swindled out of his contract to serve as Garrett's ghostwriter.

The Authentic Life of Billy, the Kid has been described by self-proclaimed Billy the Kid and Pat Garrett experts Frederick Nolan and Leon C. Metz as filled with errors, misinterpretations, and blatant lies. Nolan states that, "Far from setting the record straight, far more than all the dime novels and all the newspaper hyperbole ... *Authentic Life* has been responsible for nearly every single one of the myths perpetuated about Billy the Kid." Nolan describes Garrett's book as a "farrago of nonsense" and writes that it contains "careless inaccuracy, slanted historical accounting, deliberate untruth, and downright cover-up. . . ." Nolan adds that the publication is "a fanciful account," filled with "untruths." Though long acknowledged as unreliable, Garrett's book continued to serve as the primary source of information and inspiration for the published accounts of Billy the Kid and his deeds.

Authentic Life was clearly written, in large part, to build Billy the Kid up into a fearless and notorious outlaw, a killer of men, a man of considerable gun-fighting talents, and more. This was a calculated move to make Garrett appear heroic, brave, and determined, a lawman pitting himself against the dangerous, evil, and murderous Billy the Kid in the pursuit of justice.

During the lifetimes of Garrett, Upson, and Greene, *Authentic Life* never made any money. Upson was angered that Garrett was listed as the sole author. Sales of the book in New Mexico were particularly disappointing. According to author A. M. Gibson, "the maudlin sentimentality of many New Mexicans for Billy the Kid had made his killer, Pat Garrett, one of the most hated men in the territory." The relationship between Garrett and Upson grew strained, and the former newspaperman eventually faded from the scene, at least for a time.

In the more than a century that has passed since its publication, close analyses of *Authentic Life* have done little for Garrett's credibility; they achieved quite the opposite. It is clear that many of the published accomplishments of Pat Garrett were largely exaggerated by Upson, if not made up altogether. The fact that Garrett's name was attached to the book as author, however, made him ultimately responsible for every word in the text. Assuming Garrett read the manuscript for *Authentic Life* before it was published, he would have had ample opportunity to correct the many falsehoods contained therein, lies and misrepresentations that he must have known would come back to haunt him. He made no such effort. It causes one to wonder if Garrett ever read the book that bears his name.

It was not long after the Fort Sumner shooting that Garrett again found himself in the position of having his credibility and veracity questioned; he must have known that the very citizens who once elected him to a position of law enforcement were now turning their backs on him. Garrett began casting about for other opportunities. As usual, Garrett was out of money, and the job of sheriff did not pay enough to allow him to pursue his vices to the degree he found necessary. Garrett's life entered into a period of rapid transition.

CHAPTER 11
TRANSITIONS

PAT GARRETT DECIDED HE WOULD NOT RUN FOR ANOTHER TERM as sheriff of Lincoln County. Many believed Garrett would lose the election, and Garrett may have presumed that he could live well off the anticipated royalties from *Authentic Life*. This was not to be, as the publication was a financial disaster.

Casting about for something to do, Garrett decided to back Lincoln businessman James J. Dolan in his bid for sheriff. Garrett was inclined to cultivate relationships with politicians and prominent businessmen, and Dolan was available and close by. In time, however, Dolan's interest in running for the office faded and John Poe, Garrett's former deputy, was convinced to run instead. Poe, well liked by the community, won the election easily. According to author Metz, Poe proved to be an "incredibly efficient" lawman in stark contrast to Garrett, who had been described as "thoroughly inept" when it came to maintaining the office.

In searching for different horizons, Garrett directed his attention beyond local politics toward area and state issues. Around this time, the US Congress ordered New Mexico to reapportion, a process whereby the determination of the number of members in the US House of Representatives is based on the population of the state relative to the total US population. The responsibility for this fell to the New Mexico Territorial Legislature, but they never addressed it. The job was shifted to the recently elected New Mexico governor Lionel A. Sheldon, along with the president of the Territorial Council and the Speaker of the House of Representatives. By the time they finished with the project, Pat Garrett found himself a resident of the Ninth Council District that included Doña Ana, Grant, and Lincoln Counties. Preparations were made to elect two councilmen. The names of John A. Miller and David G. Easton were placed in nomination by the *Rio Grande Republican*. Caring little for these two men, Garrett organized a special convention for the purpose of nominating a so-called People's Ticket of officers. The convention was held on August 22, 1882, and Garrett was nominated. The *Rio Grande Republican* reported on the meeting but chose to ignore any of its nominees, mentioning only Miller and Easton as candidates. The article never mentioned Garrett, but in a separate one, the newspaper attacked the former lawman, calling him "illiterate" and "lacking in gratitude," this latter comment related to the fact that Miller and Easton once supported Garrett in his earlier election.

A number of letters subsequently published in area newspapers were critical of Garrett. Suspecting a Lincoln attorney named W. M. Roberts of writing one such letter, Garrett spotted him in town on the morning of September 19 and confronted him. Roberts denied any involvement, but Garrett kept pressuring him. Roberts responded by calling Garrett a "goddamned liar," whereupon the former sheriff pulled his revolver from its holster and whipped Roberts across the head, leaving him lying unconscious and bleeding in the street.

By the time the polls closed, the results showed Garrett losing the election by only a few votes, with most of his opposition coming from Doña Ana and Grant Counties. He had received little to no support from newspapers.

During the following months, Garrett tried to maintain a presence in politics by occasionally serving as a delegate to the capital at Santa Fe. All the while, he continued to keep his eyes open for other opportunities.

One such opportunity came Garrett's way in the form of the Texas Panhandle Cattlemen's Association. The organization approached Pat Garrett and invited him to head a company of rangers to combat the growing problem of cattle rustling. Once again in need of money, Garrett jumped at the chance to make some. At first, this quasi law enforcement organization was called the Home Rangers, but in a short time was referred to by all as the Pat Garrett Rangers. Some writers claimed that Garrett was awarded a commission from Texas governor John Ireland, but no such document has ever been found. Promised a salary of $5,000 per year, Garrett wasted no time in assembling a group of men to facilitate meeting the needs of the stockmen.

Garrett was initially called in by the cattlemen's association to solve a problem that started with water resources. The larger cattle ranches were growing concerned about the smaller ranchers moving into the area and competing for the already limited water supply. Coupled with this was the additional pressing concern that Panhandle cowhands were moving closer to striking for higher wages and seeking a greater economic independence.

The cattlemen associated with the large ranchers took to fencing off prized waterholes and even posting guards to keep the smaller ranchers away. As the smaller ranchers found it difficult to impossible to water their cattle, many of them eventually sold out to the larger ones. As the larger ranches expanded and appeared to earn greater profits, cowhands were still paid only $25 to $30 per month for working from dawn to dark and beyond. They were provided two meals per day, were never compensated for injuries (which were common), and were often not paid until cattle were delivered to market weeks later and after a long trail drive. Further, a large percentage of the cowhands were in debt to their employers because they were initially supplied with saddles, blankets, and other important items. The hired hands signed a promissory note for these items and money for them was deducted from forthcoming paychecks.

The cowhands found themselves short on money more often than not, and some of them had families to support. As a result, many of them took to a process called "mavericking," whereby the cowhands would round up dozens and sometimes hundreds of unbranded stray cattle and apply their own brand to them. In the Panhandle, some of the larger ranchers began accusing the cowhands of separating unbranded calves from their mothers and marking them with their own brand. This was regarded as a form of rustling.

The cattlemen's association ordered a halt to any and all private or unauthorized branding on land controlled by them. This slowed but did not stop the rustling. Because cowhands found it more difficult to pursue a potential living via mavericking, they decided to demand higher wages. During the first part of 1883, twenty-five cowhands drafted and signed a document that stated they would not work for less than $50 per month. One line in the document read, "Anyone violating the above considerations shall suffer the consequences."

An attempt at compromise was put forth by a couple of the larger ranches, but was turned down. Approximately one hundred cowhands decided to go on strike and by doing so forced the hands of the larger ranchers. Initially, the plan backfired.

The names of all of the striking cowhands were published and distributed throughout the Panhandle area with the warning that they were not to be hired by anyone. Most ranchers agreed not to hire any man whose name appeared on the list. A number of the striking cowhands decided to move to New Mexico to seek employment. Others decided to join them, but before leaving, accumulated a herd of several hundred head of cattle, all rustled from their former employers. A number of early New Mexico ranches were started with rustled Texas cattle, and a handful of these were in Lincoln County.

The group of men Garrett assembled to pursue and arrest the rustlers was a questionable lot. Jim East, the well-respected and popular sheriff of Oldham County, stated that he would have nothing to do with the Pat Garrett Rangers, and expressed surprise at the type of men selected. East described them all as "heavy drinkers and vindictive." A number of them were believed to have been engaged in rustling livestock in the past.

During the days that followed, the Pat Garrett Rangers pursued rustlers throughout much of the Texas Panhandle. Several arrests were made, but they were mostly for violations of a handgun law. It soon became clear that the intent of the arrest warrants and the handgun stricture was to frighten out of the area those men the big ranchers deemed undesirable. In the process, the Garrett Rangers antagonized and alienated the majority of Panhandle residents. A number of citizens opposed the rangers to the point of taking up arms against them, and what author Metz called "private wars" broke out between Garrett's men and area cowhands.

In early 1885, Garrett's enthusiasm for his assignment was waning. According to writers Leon Metz and Emerson Hough, Garrett was likely disillusioned by the suspicion that his employers were more interested in having their enemies killed or run out of the country than in bringing them to justice. Garrett disbanded the rangers in the spring of the year and decided to return to ranching.

After leaving the Pat Garrett Rangers assignment in the Texas Panhandle, Garrett returned to his New Mexico ranch and, for a time, committed himself to making a success of it. He ran cattle and horses. He was more interested in the horses than the cattle, for he often raced his stock and took pride in their breeding. Unfortunately, he lost as much or more as he won. As Garrett pursued ranching, it became increasingly clear that he was not cut out for it. While he possessed the necessary knowledge and experience to become a successful rancher, Garrett was more inclined to spend his time drinking, gambling, and whoring. In addition, his ever-growing ego demanded that he remain in the public eye. Ranching for Garrett turned out to be yet another failure, and once again, he was desperately in need of funds. In time, a new opportunity arose.

During a visit to Tascosa, Texas, Garrett met a man named Captain Brandon Kirby. Kirby served as an agent who represented Scotsmen who were interested in establishing ranches in the American West. During this time, Scots, along with British and Irish, were investing in western cattle ranches. Garrett agreed to work as a subagent for Kirby and identify some choice ranch properties for prospective buyers. In effect, Garrett was to be a real estate agent. During the ensuing months, Garrett assisted Kirby in closing on several ranch properties. Garrett even sold his own holdings at a good price. A short time later, he purchased another ranch in the area.

Kirby was funded by, worked for, and reported to a man named James Cree, a wealthy Scotsman. Cree himself had moved to a large ranch in New Mexico and assigned Kirby as ranch manager. Garrett was placed on a retainer to provide timely assistance. Cree, who regarded himself as royalty and above reproach, treated his ranch hands with disdain and considered them members of the peasant class. The cowhands resented the poor treatment, and in retaliation they rustled dozens of newborn calves. In addition to the cowhands, Cree's neighbors cared little for the hostile treatment they received from the Scotsman. They not only had little to nothing to do with him, they, like some of Cree's cowhands, rustled some of his cattle.

In need of replacing the rustled cattle, Cree imported 150 Black Angus bulls from Scotland. He was convinced that the new stock would increase production and improve the quality of beef. By this time, however, Cree had angered and antagonized so many of his cowhands and neighbors that they were determined to see him fail. Several neighboring ranchers castrated most of the bulls. They were assisted in this effort by Cree's own cowhands. As if this weren't bad enough, things were about to get worse.

In addition to the loss of livestock via rustling, along with problems associated with blizzards and hail, one of the worst droughts in history descended on Lincoln County in 1886 and all of the waterholes on Cree's ranch dried up. Hundreds of his Angus cattle died from thirst. Unable to survive all of his difficulties, Cree and his family returned to Scotland.

With Cree out of the country, Garrett was once again out of a job and pondered his next move. Having observed the effects of the drought, Garrett hit on the idea of developing an irrigation project that would provide necessary water for ranchers and make a lot of badly needed money for himself.

Following the end of his venture into real estate, Pat Garrett moved onto another of his holdings—an eighteen-hundred-acre ranch and farm located east of Roswell, New Mexico, in the Pecos River Valley. In addition to cattle, Garrett oversaw an orchard of apples, peaches, and pecans, as well as a vineyard and a vast field of alfalfa. From all appearances, it looked as though Garrett had it made. Garrett identified himself to others as a prosperous rancher/farmer.

In truth, however, Garrett was anything but prosperous. Garrett had no more enthusiasm for ranching and farming this time around than he did previously. His crops and herd went neglected. His profits, if they existed at all, were marginal. Garrett's continued pursuit of his vices used up what little money he had, and he began to seek income from a new enterprise that involved irrigation.

Author Metz, a Garrett apologist, described the former lawman as a visionary who longed to see the Pecos River Valley "flourish with crops, with businesses, with schools." For these arid sandy wastes to flourish, they had to have water, and that meant irrigation ditches and canals to distribute the precious commodity throughout the area. Without water, agriculture would be marginal to impossible. Unfortunately, irrigation cost money, and Garrett had none.

In an attempt to lure settlers into the region, the Territory of New Mexico passed legislation in 1887 that provided opportunities for people to form companies oriented toward the construction and maintenance of reservoirs and canals, as well as ditches and pipelines, for the purpose of irrigation, mining, and manufacturing. The legislation encouraged such companies to raise money via the sale of stock. Garrett viewed this new opportunity as his shortcut to wealth and power.

On January 15, 1887, Garrett agreed to purchase one-third of a business called the Texas Irrigation Ditch Company. The owner was a Roswell businessman named William M. Holloman. By August 15, the company had been renamed the Holloman and Garrett Ditch Company. The company's source of water was to come from the North Spring River, which was located on Garrett's ranch. No records of this company have ever been located, and a short time after its formation it disappeared.

After this, Garrett purchased a one-sixteenth interest in the Pioneer Ditch Company from another Roswell businessman named Thomas B. Zumwalt. Since Garrett had no money, it is likely that the "purchase" was an in-kind agreement. Like the previous venture, the Pioneer Ditch Company dissolved after a few weeks, having accomplished nothing.

Following these two failures, Garrett decided to organize his own irrigation company. He determined that it was possible to construct a dam a mile-and-a-half below the junction of the Rio Hondo and Berrendo Creek, thereby capturing the flow of the two streams. Once the reservoir was filled, the water would be distributed via canals. When a consistent supply of irrigation water could be assured, the normally arid sand hills could be offered for sale. Garrett was convinced he could make money not only by selling water rights, but by selling land as well. To make it all work, however, Garrett needed financing. He found a source of funding from Charles B. Eddy, a prominent New Mexico cattle rancher who knew less about irrigation than Garrett.

On July 18, 1887, Garrett and Eddy were joined by Charles Greene (the publisher of Garrett's unsuccessful book) to form the Pecos Valley Irrigation and Investment Company (PVI&IC). Greene was to be the general manager, and Garrett and Eddy would handle promotion, sales, and the granting of ditch rights. Greene made several trips to Chicago to solicit potential investors in the company. Several major stockholders came on board and the company boasted assets of $600,000. The PVI&IC bought out another ditch company and took possession of the Northern Canal, which stretched over forty miles with a number of waterways and pipelines connected to it. More construction was undertaken, and soon it became clear that the PVI&IC had underestimated the costs. As a result, the company soon found itself on the verge of running out of money before the project was completed.

Charles Eddy made a trip to Colorado Springs, Colorado, to invite Punch Cigar magnate Robert Weems Tansill to invest in the PVI&IC. Tansill agreed, and in turn invited friend and fellow businessman James John Hagerman to assume control of the company. Hagerman, whose background included a wide experience in constructing railroads, agreed. The arrival of Hagerman, however, spelled doom for Pat Garrett.

Hagerman disliked Garrett from the outset, regarded him as considerably less than a social peer, and referred to him as "half-educated." Hagerman reorganized the PVI&IC and renamed it the Pecos Valley Irrigation and Improvement Company. Garrett was left entirely out of the reorganization. Once again, he was out of a job and broke.

Garrett returned to his ranch. After six years of investing and promoting irrigation schemes, he was no better off than when he started. He was in need of a way to earn some income. More importantly, he was in need of a means to continue to be Pat Garrett, the man and the image he believed he had become.

After considerable wrangling, it was decided by the New Mexico Territorial Legislature to divide Lincoln County into two separate counties. Roswell residents had been lobbying for such for some time. Roswell lay sixty miles east of the town of Lincoln, the county seat, and citizens complained about having to travel that distance to conduct business related to registering a deed, securing a marriage license, or serving on a jury. The logistics were annoying, inconvenient, and often created hardship.

The new county, which would establish Roswell as the county seat, was to be named Chaves County after Colonel J. Francisco

Chavez. Anglo citizens of the new county were troubled at the notion of it being named after a non-white. An odd compromise resulted: The name was accepted but the spelling was changed from Chavez to Chaves.

The initial Chaves County officials were appointed by the state legislature. Elections were scheduled for 1890, and hopeful candidates were beginning to lay groundwork for their campaigns. Notable among the Democratic candidates was Pat Garrett, who was convinced he would be elected the first sheriff of Chaves County. Given Garrett's ego, he assumed he would be unopposed once word got around that he was running for the position. He was unprepared and surprised, therefore, to learn that he had an opponent—his former deputy, John W. Poe. Rather than run against Poe in the Democratic primary, Garrett decided to run as an independent. He was soundly defeated.

UVALDE, TEXAS

Garrett was angered and bitter at his defeat. He was now aware that the tide of public opinion had shifted and that he was no longer perceived as the hero, the fearless lawman, he believed himself to be. He decided it was time for him to leave New Mexico. After disposing of his holdings, Garrett and his family set out for Uvalde, Texas, in April 1891. Uvalde was located one hundred miles west of San Antonio. Accompanying the Garretts was Ashmon Upson. In spite of Upson's position that Garrett wrote none of the book *Authentic Life*, the two managed to remain friends.

On settling in at Uvalde, Garrett was determined to renew his plans to promote and manage irrigation activities, but as he was broke and unable to entice area businessmen to back his venture, his plans never got off the ground. Garrett spent most of his time with Upson drinking, gambling, and racing horses. Somehow, Garrett again managed to purchase a ranch. When he was not cavorting with Upson, the former lawman managed to spend more time with his family. Life in Uvalde was relatively peaceful for Garrett, though he always remained on the edge of bankruptcy. While he managed to pass the days in this relatively peaceful community, Garrett missed the excitement of law enforcement, missed the praise and adulation he received when he was perceived as a successful lawman. Little did he know that another opportunity to be in the public light would soon come his way. This opportunity, however, was one that placed Garrett on the road to his ultimate fate.

PART II
SETTING THE STAGE

CHAPTER 12

ENTER COLONEL ALBERT JENNINGS FOUNTAIN

WHILE PAT GARRETT WAS RESIDING ON HIS RANCH IN UVALDE, a man named Colonel Albert Jennings Fountain was making headlines in New Mexico. The two men were soon to be intertwined in a growing web of intrigue that was to become one of the greatest mysteries in the American West. On February 1, 1896, Colonel Fountain and his nine-year-old son Henry vanished somewhere along a road that wound though a portion of New Mexico's White Sands and were never seen again. The disappearance captured the attention of the nation and remained the most talked about disappearance until aviatrix Amelia Earhart vanished somewhere in the Pacific Ocean in 1937.

Albert Jennings Fountain was born on October 23, 1838, on Staten Island, New York. He was born Albert Jennings but later took on the surname Fountain, which was derived from his mother's relatives named de la Fontaine. Fountain arrived in California during the early 1850s and found a job as a reporter for the *Sacramento Union*. While living in California, Fountain sometimes worked as a law clerk, and eventually passed the California state bar exam.

Col. Albert Jennings Fountain
RICHARD KOLB

At the advent of the Civil War, Fountain enlisted in Company E of the First California Infantry Volunteers. Later while stationed in New Mexico, Fountain married Mariana Lopez on October 27, 1862. In time the couple produced ten children.

When his term in military service was up, Fountain reenlisted and spent most of his remaining time in the army pursuing renegade Navajo Indians. During one engagement he was wounded and sent to El Paso, Texas, to recover. Fountain became enamored of the city and decided to move his family there. After settling in, he established a law practice and joined the Masonic Lodge. In 1869, Fountain was elected to the Texas State Senate.

In 1873, Fountain and his family moved to Mesilla, New Mexico, and into Mariana's former home. Here, Fountain built another law practice. In 1881, he was appointed by the court to defend the outlaw Billy the Kid for the murder of Sheriff William Brady in Lincoln. He lost the case. Later, Fountain was named an assistant US district attorney. In addition, he was a member of the Mesilla Scouts, a local militia that had the responsibility of defending the town against Indian raids and cattle rustling. In 1883, Fountain attained the rank of colonel in the militia.

In 1887, Fountain established the *Mesilla Valley Independent*, an unapologetically Republican-leaning newspaper. He wrote blistering columns condemning those who did not ascribe to his philosophies as well as praising himself and his service to the country during his military enlistment. It is believed by many that Fountain's heroic accounts of his daring military adventures were exaggerated. Like politicians everywhere, Fountain possessed a lofty self-image.

Fountain became a prominent member of the Mesilla community, active not only in law and politics, but also in church, education, and expanding cultural opportunities. As he was being touted as a potential leader in area and state politics, his star was clearly on the rise. Fountain envisioned few if any obstacles to his path, until the arrival of a man who was to become one of his most formidable foes and hated enemies—Albert Bacon Fall.

CHAPTER 13
ENTER ALBERT BACON FALL

THE YEAR 1887 ALSO SAW THE ARRIVAL OF ALBERT BACON FALL in New Mexico. A Kentucky native, Fall set up his own law practice and served as an attorney for the Democratic Party. The two Alberts—Fall and Fountain—both of them strong-willed, temperamental, ruthless, and egocentric—were destined to collide, and before much time passed each was dedicated to the notion of bringing down the other.

Albert Fall possessed southern loyalties and Fountain was a dedicated Yankee. Even though the Civil War had been over for more than two decades, feelings still ran high and there was little mixing between the two political and cultural camps. In New Mexico, Fountain, by virtue of his age, experience, and a number of successes, was regarded as a political power. Fall, on the other hand, was young, energetic, and longed for the prestige and power manifested by Fountain. Fall immediately saw Fountain as an adversary. Fountain, sensing competition from this new rival, was determined to maintain his position and do whatever was necessary to assure that end.

Fountain counted among his supporters the members of the Mexican community of Mesilla. This resulted, in part, because he was married to a Mexican, but also, and perhaps more importantly, he successfully represented the ethnic group in court to a variety of successes. As a result of this relationship, many Anglos felt they were not being adequately represented by Fountain and sought help from outside the Republican Party. Fall noted this and perceived it would lead to increasing difficulties for Fountain on the political front. Fall decided it was time to move into Fountain's domain and begin to take control. He relocated to Las Cruces, the town immediately north of Mesilla, and in a short time founded his own newspaper, the *Independent Democrat*. It was not long before the two men were battling with one another via editorials in their respective newspapers.

In the next election, Fountain and Fall ran for a seat in the New Mexico House of Representatives. The race was close, and Fountain won by a tiny margin. Following the election, Fountain departed for the capital—Santa Fe—where he was soon elected Speaker of the House.

Fall was disappointed in the election result, but more than that, he was embarrassed. He rationalized his defeat by attributing it to the fact that Fountain had been in the area longer and was more widely known. Fall was determined to change all of that. Within weeks of the election, Fall busied himself with examining ways to win the next race. While immersed in this quest, he met Oliver Milton Lee, an area rancher with the reputation of one who always got what he wanted, though sometimes trampling adversaries in the process. In time, the two men together would evolve into the chief adversaries of Pat Garrett.

CHAPTER 14
ENTER OLIVER LEE

OLIVER MILTON LEE WAS A RANCHER WHO OWNED A LARGE parcel of land on the western slope of the Sacramento Mountains near Dog Canyon. The Sacramentos are seventy miles northeast of El Paso, Texas, and thirty miles southeast of Alamogordo, New Mexico. Lee and his family arrived in the area during the early 1880s from Texas, bringing with them a great herd of cattle. Though unproven at the time, it was believed by many southeastern New Mexico residents that Lee built up his herd by rustling stock from his neighbors. Lee was also handy with a gun, possessed a violent streak, and had killed men. When the time came that Lee had need of a lawyer, he saw something he liked in Albert B. Fall. Both men operated within the structure of the law when necessary, but when the law interfered with their advancement, they were more than willing to step outside its boundaries.

As Lee and Fall became more acquainted, the rancher was invited to assist with Fall's political ambitions. During the 1892 elections, Fall had gained such a great deal of momentum and recognition that the Republicans grew worried. In response, they called for the state militia to oversee the polls. Fall responded to this move by sending Oliver Lee and his most trusted gunmen as a countermove. Among his gunmen were Bill McNew, Jim

Oliver Milton Lee
RICHARD KOLB

Gilliland, and Todd Bailey—three men who, in addition to Lee and Fall, were destined to impact the life of Pat Garrett.

During the night, Lee's men arrived in Las Cruces and took up positions on rooftops, weapons at the ready. The following morning, the state militia, led by Major W. H. H. Llewellyn and Captain Thomas Brannigan, made their way down the street on horseback. Fall exited an establishment and stepped out in the middle of the roadway to confront them. He ordered Llewellyn to turn the militia around and leave town or they would be killed. He then pointed to Lee and his armed men on the rooftops, all of whom were aiming rifles at the troopers. Unprepared for this turn of events, Llewellyn and his men milled about for a few minutes and then departed.

When the votes were finally tallied, the Democrats emerged as victors. The election outcome was challenged by the Republicans, but nothing was changed. Fall had made his mark in a sensational way, and the voters would not soon forget.

CHAPTER 15
ENTER TODD BAILEY

Over the years, Oliver Lee had surrounded himself with competent gunmen, men who had no qualms about shooting a suspected rustler, or even someone who interfered in one way or another with Lee's plans to advance his cattle ranching empire. Jim Gilliland, Bill McNew, Ed Brown, and others were among these men, but if Lee had a favorite, one he could depend on to remain loyal to him and to carry out any order, no matter how illegal or immoral it might be, it was Todd Bailey.

For reasons no one completely understands, Todd Bailey has never occupied a position in western American history alongside Pat Garrett, Oliver Lee, and other notables of the time. As events in southeastern New Mexico progressed, Bailey became a significant and important, though understated, figure and was to assume a major role in the assassinations of Colonel Albert Jennings Fountain and Pat Garrett, as well as others. It concerns serious researchers and investigators that historians dropped the ball on this noteworthy and major character in the unfolding events. For more on Todd Bailey, see the Appendix.

Charles Lewis Bailey was born on July 12, 1879, in Buffalo Gap, Texas, to Rutha Altman and John Wesley Bailey. A younger sister gave him the nickname "Todd." Bailey's mother was the older half-sister of Oliver Lee. Todd's older brother, named Oliver, was named for Oliver Lee's father. When young Oliver Bailey was seven years of age, he was killed in a wagon accident. Todd was only two years old at the time. Rutha died two years later, leaving Todd and his sister Mamie to be raised by their father, who a short time later moved the family to Commerce, Texas. One published account has John Wesley Bailey dying from a heart attack three-and-a-half years later and the children placed with a neighbor. According to Bailey family history, however, John Wesley simply dropped the children off at the home of their uncle Charlie Haas and his wife and rode away.

Life for the Bailey children at the Haas farm was far from pleasant. Charlie Haas worked the young ones from dawn until dusk and treated them poorly, often whipping them at the slightest irritation. Todd despised his uncle, but options were few for the orphan.

Far away in New Mexico, Mary Lee, Oliver's mother, learned that her grandchildren were being treated harshly by Haas and his wife. She sent her son Oliver to Commerce to retrieve them and bring them to the New Mexico ranch. Oliver Lee made the journey, but succeeded in returning with only one of the children, Mamie. It was never learned why the other child—Todd—was left behind.

On July 6, 1890, when Todd Bailey was a few days short of his eleventh birthday and six years from the day they were dropped off at the Haas farm, John Wesley Bailey rode up to the Commerce home. On spotting his father, Todd likely thought he had come to rescue him from his hated uncle, but it was not to be. Without speaking to anyone, the elder Bailey unsaddled his horse, walked over to the front porch without acknowledging anyone's presence, and threw his saddle to the ground. After stretching for a moment, he lay down, using the saddle for a pillow, and died.

One afternoon when Haas thought Todd was not working hard enough, he lashed him with a horsewhip, opening cuts on his face and chest. The boy fell against a wagon wheel where he was pinned and unable to flee. Haas continued lashing with vigor. Todd tried to roll away and wound up on top of a pitchfork as the whip snapped across his back. He was certain his uncle was trying to kill him.

From the ground, Todd seized the pitchfork and thrust it upward, hard, and plunged it into his uncle's stomach and deep into the rib cage. Haas dropped to the ground, blood pouring from his wound and puddling on the hay-covered ground. Through his tears, Todd Bailey watched his hated uncle writhing on the ground, moaning in pain. He turned and ran, his only thought to get as far from the Haas farm as possible. He stopped at a shallow creek some distance away long enough to ponder what he had done. He realized he could never go back, so he continued running.

From Commerce, Todd fled to Abilene in the hope of finding some Altman and Lee relatives only to learn that they had all moved to New Mexico. With only vague information about where the Lees had relocated, the youngster somehow made his away across seven hundred miles of arid and sparsely populated West Texas and into the rolling New Mexico plains near the Sacramento Mountains. Weeks later, he arrived at the doorstep of the Lee ranch house, nearly dead from starvation. Here, Todd was reunited with his sister Mamie, and the two were raised by their loving grandmother, Mary.

As he grew up, Todd Bailey learned ranching and cowboy skills from his uncle Oliver Lee, who served as mentor, protector, and surrogate parent. Todd soon became one of the ranch's most capable and dependable hands. In addition, while still in his early teens, he worked as an agent for Lee, selling horses for him from time to time.

There was never a ranch hand more devoted and loyal to Oliver Lee than Todd Bailey. Were it not for Lee and grandmother Mary, Todd would not have found a home and his survival would have been in question. He owed much to them both. To Todd Bailey, Oliver Lee was everything—his inspiration, his hero, and there was nothing he would not do for his uncle.

In addition to introducing his nephew Todd to ranching and related skills, Oliver Lee also provided instruction in the use of firearms. By this time, Lee was perceived by many as a dangerous gunman and a sure shot. It was related that Lee could toss a silver dollar into the air, draw his revolver, and pierce it with a bullet before it hit the ground. Such accounts about the shooting skills of western figures abound and most of them are either exaggerated or outright lies, but this demonstration of marksmanship by Lee had been observed and reported on. Todd was a capable student, and in time his skills rivaled, even exceeded, those of his teacher, abilities that were to come in handy for Oliver Lee within a few years.

Todd Bailey went to his grave believing he had killed his uncle, Charlie Haas. Investigative efforts yielded the information that, though badly wounded, Haas recovered. Years later he moved to Victoria, Texas, where he lived out the rest of his life.

CHAPTER 16

TULAROSA AND MESILLA VALLEY TROUBLES

Politics and the growing conflict between Albert Jennings Fountain and Albert Bacon Fall provided a slight distraction from the serious problems with which residents of the Tularosa and Mesilla Valleys were forced to contend. As a result of the arid environment and frequent dry seasons, water and grazing rights remained vital to the livelihood of area ranchers and farmers. The courts were often filled with cases involving challenges to water holes and stream entitlements. The availability of water determined whether or not a rancher or farmer succeeded or failed.

Tularosa Valley was also home to desperate men and a criminal element. Shootings were not uncommon in the area, and these exchanges of gunfire often resulted in the death of one or more of the participants. Oliver Lee and his gunmen were ubiquitous during these times. Lee had been targeted by a number of Tularosa Valley ranchers as a man who expanded his herd by rustling the livestock of others. In an ironic turnabout, once Lee had established one of the largest herds in the valley, he became the target of rustlers. His ranch hands, all competent gunmen, had orders to shoot and kill cattle thieves on sight. During the winter of 1893, Lee spotted Matt Coffelt and Charles Rhodius stealing cattle from a portion of his ranch, He shot and killed them both. When brought into court, Lee entered a plea of self-defense and was acquitted.

In March 1894, twenty-one New Mexico cattle ranchers gathered to discuss ways to halt what they perceived as a rustling epidemic. They met in Las Cruces and formed the Southeastern New Mexico Livestock Association. Oliver Lee signed on as a member. Colonel Albert Jennings Fountain was named the association's lawyer, and very little time passed before he was prosecuting rustlers. Several of the convicted rustlers were sentenced to prison terms; others were directed to leave the state. Despite the efforts of Fountain and the cattlemen's association, however, the rustling continued unabated.

Unknown to Oliver Lee at the time, Fountain regarded him as one of the principal rustlers in the area. On the sly, Fountain accumulated evidence and testimony from Lee's neighbors who claimed the rancher had rustled everything from a single cow to an entire herd. Lee was suspected of rustling and either selling or butchering hundreds of head of cattle. The neighbors told Fountain that they were not inclined to confront Lee for they knew him to be a hardened killer who was normally surrounded by his gunmen, including McNew, Gilliland, and Bailey. They felt they had little recourse except to rely on the livestock association.

When Fountain learned that Albert Fall was Lee's attorney, it added an element of revenge to the efforts of the colonel. Fountain was devoted to ending rustling in that part of New Mexico, and in the process he considered that he might very well interrupt Fall's promising political career.

A cattle detective named Les Dow was hired to gather evidence on Lee. Dow took a job at one of the large ranches and participated in a group roundup near the Sacramento Mountains. He had an informer on his payroll who told him that there was a stolen and rebranded steer in the Lee-McNew herd. Dow spotted a steer with a suspicious brand. He approached McNew and offered to purchase it for $20. McNew took the money and Dow herded the steer to an isolated area, killed it, and skinned it. On the inside of the hide, Dow discovered that the brand had been altered to match Lee's. Dow immediately reported the discovery to Fountain, and the attorney decided to charge Lee with rustling.

Fountain considered that if he brought down Lee, Albert Fall would soon follow. While Fountain was good at his job, he was not fully cognizant of the fact that Lee and Fall, along with their cadre of gunmen and politicos, were determined, vengeful, deadly, and not shy about taking what they wanted, whatever the cost.

On the morning of January 12, Fountain hitched up a buckboard and prepared to leave Mesilla for the courthouse at Lincoln to obtain the necessary indictments against Lee. The roads to Lincoln wound through largely unpopulated and sparsely traveled areas, and Fountain expressed some apprehension that men might be out to get him. Fountain's wife, Mariana, sensed her husband's concern that an attempt might be made on his life, so she insisted that he take along their eight-year-old son, Henry. Mariana was convinced that no one would perpetrate any kind of evil with a child along. Mariana would live to regret her decision.

Though the sun was shining, the morning was bitterly cold. Fountain and Henry wrapped themselves in blankets against the low temperatures and the bitter wind. After leaving Mesilla, they traveled northeastward through San Augustin Pass, past Chalk Hill in the White Sands, then onto Pellman's Well, La Luz, Tularosa, and finally arrived in Lincoln

At the courthouse, cattle detective Les Dow displayed the cowhide showing the brand that had been altered in Lee's favor. Several ranchers who had been invited to the hearing provided testimony against Lee and others. By the time the session wound down, thirty-two indictments were handed down. Two of them were Case No. 1489, *Territory of New Mexico v. William McNew and Oliver Lee*, a charge of cattle theft, and Case No. 1890, *Territory of New Mexico v. William McNew and Oliver Lee*, a charge of defacing brands.

With the session concluded, Fountain was making plans to leave when a man he had never seen before stepped up to him and handed him a note. It read: "IF YOU DROP THIS CASE WE WILL BE YOUR FRIENDS. IF YOU GO WITH IT YOU WILL NEVER REACH HOME ALIVE."

It wasn't until the afternoon of January 30 that Fountain and son Henry left Lincoln. They drove for eighteen miles and arrived at the home of J. H. Blazer in Mescalero where father and son spent the night. Blazer was an old friend and welcomed his guests. While they visited, Fountain expressed concerns for his safety, but was determined to press on toward Mesilla. Shortly after dawn the following morning, Fountain and Henry bade goodbye to Blazer and set out toward the southwest. Fountain hadn't been on the road for more than ten minutes when he noticed two men on horseback following him. They were too far away for him to see their faces. By the end of the day, Fountain pulled the buckboard into the yard of a friend in La Luz, a few miles south of Tularosa. There, they spent the night.

On Saturday, February 1, Fountain and Henry departed La Luz and headed for home. Twenty-five miles later as they approached Chalk Hill near the White Sands, Fountain glanced behind him and spotted three men following at a distance. Around noon, Fountain pulled the buckboard to a halt and visited for several minutes with Santos Alvarado, who was carrying mail from Las Cruces to Tularosa. During their conversation, Fountain told Alvarado about the trio of men following him. Following a bit more conversation, the two friends bade goodbye to one another and Fountain continued on toward Pellman's Well, a short distance away. At the well there was an opportunity to take a short break and water the horses. This done, Fountain got back on the road for the leg of the journey that would take him over Chalk Hill, through San Augustin Pass, and thence to Mesilla.

A few minutes after leaving Pellman's Well, Fountain encountered another mail carrier, Saturnino Barela. Barela noticed the three men following Fountain and encouraged the lawyer to accompany him to Luna's Well, spend the night there, and then travel on to Mesilla in the morning. Fountain thought about the offer, but explained to Barela that Henry was getting a cold and that he wanted to get him home where his mother could take care of him. The two men said their farewells and rode their separate ways. It was the last time anyone except the killers saw Albert Jennings Fountain and his son alive.

The sun was descending toward the western horizon as Fountain approached Chalk Hill. With around two hours of daylight remaining, he hoped to make San Augustin Pass before dark. From there, the remainder of the trip would be relatively short and downhill.

The desert landscape here is open and flat for miles around, the views wide and expansive. Yucca, creosote, and clumps of brush dot the relatively featureless environment. Here and there, slight variations in the landscape occur, one of which was Chalk Hill. Chalk Hill is not so much a hill as it is a slight rise in the otherwise featureless plain. Not far away toward the north was White Sands, an extensive array of weathered gypsum sands the persistent desert winds had formed into spectacular, shining dunes, a remnant of an ancient sea bottom.

As Fountain steered the buckboard toward Chalk Hill, it is likely that he still carried the Winchester across his lap. Henry was perched to his right on the wooden spring seat. The dispatch case carrying the indictments for Oliver Lee and other cattle rustlers was riding under the seat.

As the buckboard crested Chalk Hill, Fountain saw nothing or no one, least of all the man who was hidden in a clump of brush several yards south of the hill and off to his left. The man was Todd Bailey, the nephew of Oliver Lee. Bailey had proven himself an excellent marksman and had been enlisted by his uncle to take out his nemesis, Albert Fountain. Bailey was seventeen years old.

Not far away but out of sight, three horsemen sat in their saddles and waited for what was to come. Researchers have debated the identity of the horsemen, but most have narrowed it down to a choice between James Gilliland, Bill McNew, Ed Brown, and Oliver Lee. It has been suggested and argued that Lee was not among the three, but was stationed a short distance away. (According to Ed Brown in a statement to George Curry, Oliver Lee was involved in the plot to kill Fountain, but was not at Chalk Hill at the time of the murder.)

According to Bailey family members, as the buckboard began the descent down the gentle slope of Chalk Hill, Todd Bailey raised his rifle and sighted on Fountain. Just as the buckboard reached the bottom of the slope, he fired. The bullet from Bailey's rifle struck Fountain, a mortal wound.

An alternative version of this event exists, one credited to Jim Gilliland and related to author Leon Metz in a 1969 interview with Butler Oral Burris, a friend of Gilliland's. According to Burris, Gilliland stated that he, Oliver Lee, and Bill McNew took up pursuit of Fountain as he was arriving near the uphill (northeast) portion of Chalk Hill. All three men, using rifles, shot at Fountain, at least one bullet striking him in the back. According to Burris,

Jim Gilliland
RICHARD KOLB

Gilliland stated that Fountain "looked just like an old bullfrog when he jumped between the horses [pulling the buckboard]."

Some have questioned this second version of the attack on Fountain. For one thing, this tactic makes little sense, for the speeding wagon would have made Fountain a difficult target. It has also been argued that the intent may have been to chase Fountain to a point near Bailey, and should Bailey miss his target, the three horsemen were thus in a position to overtake the buckboard and kill Fountain. Another reason for the skepticism applied to this version is that, according to acquaintances, Gilliland was reputed to misrepresent accounts of his past on occasion.

Whatever reaction made by the dead or dying Fountain caused the team of horses to veer sharply to the left (east) where the road leveled out from the hill's slope. The horses raced another few dozen yards before stopping. According to the tracks found at the scene, three men rode up to the buckboard moments later and surrounded it. It has been suggested on the basis of tracks that they were joined by a fourth man on foot. The fourth man was likely Todd Bailey. At this point, a decision needed to be made: Eight-year-old Henry Fountain was still alive and was a witness to the killing. Seated in the buggy, he looked into the faces of the men surrounding him, men who were responsible for killing his father. In turn, the men regarded the boy, and nervously came to the realization that he would have to be dealt with.

It was imperative that the killers get the buckboard containing the presumed dead Fountain and his son far from the main road. This well-used route saw travelers, freighters, mail carriers, and others, and a rider could arrive at any minute. Taking the lead lines to Fountain's team of horses, the riders continued eastward. After traveling for much of the night, they finally reined in and set up camp at a location called Horse Camp Mesa. By the time the killers had arrived at this location, they had been joined by Oliver Lee. Here, Fountain's body was pulled from the buckboard and placed on a blanket that had been spread out on the ground nearby. The pony that had been tied to the rear of the vehicle was turned loose, and it trotted away to the north. A fire was started and a coffeepot set onto the coals.

William McNew
RICHARD KOLB

One can only imagine the terror that filled young Henry Fountain. Based on footprints later found at the scene, it was apparent that the boy was still alive at this point. Around the campsite that evening as the men drank coffee and smoked cigarettes, they discussed what must be done with Henry. The only conclusion they felt they could arrive at was to eliminate all witnesses, which meant that the boy had to be killed, a task that appealed to none of them. They decided to draw straws to determine who would execute the lad. Jim Gilliland drew the short straw.

Henry was seated not far away. It will never be known if he overheard the conversation between the men. After finishing his cigarette, Gilliland rose from his position near the fire. With his back to Henry, he withdrew a pocketknife and opened it, the three-inch blade gleaming in the firelight. Holding the knife against one leg, Gilliland casually walked away from the campfire and circled around to a point behind Henry. Without hesitating, Gilliland grabbed the boy by the hair with his left hand, pulled his head back, and slit his throat. Gilliland released his hold on Henry's hair and the boy dropped to the sandy ground, bleeding to death.

After sunrise the following day, the killers awoke, made coffee, and made plans to depart. The bodies of Albert and Henry Fountain were tied to the backs of horses. After the campfire had been doused, the riders saddled up and traveled eastward toward the Jarilla Mountains. The buckboard was left behind at Horse Camp Mesa. Close to the base of Culp Peak, located farther north in the Sacramento Mountains, was a steam-operated water pump. Adjacent to the pump was the boiler. The water pumped from the well went into a nearby tank from which cattle drank. It was to this location the riders guided their horses, their grisly cargo in tow.

The two bodies were placed inside the firebox of the boiler and a fire started. The door to the firebox was closed tightly, thus causing the oxygen to be depleted. Thus, the fire died and there was no direct flame to the bodies, just heat. The bodies were rendered; the fat melted away and the muscles and tendons shrank, causing the corpses to shrivel. The bodies remained in the boiler for the night.

The next morning, the fire door was opened. The remains were pulled out and wrapped in blankets. They were taken to Oliver Lee's Dog Canyon Ranch and buried in the peach orchard that was only a few dozen yards in front of the house. Nearby was a hog pen in which Lee kept a number of swine. Once or twice each year a few hogs were butchered, the best cuts of the meat hung in the smokehouse, and the rest turned into sausage. To disguise the grave Lee had the hogs turned loose to root around in the orchard.

Unexpectedly, the hogs rooted up the corpse of Henry Fountain at the same time that Lucy Gilliland, the sister of Jim Gilliland, stepped out of the house and walked into the orchard. She said something to her brother who, disturbed at the reappearance of the bodies, determined to relocate them. It is not clear if Gilliland informed Oliver Lee of the discovery, but since it occurred in Lee's front yard, it is presumed that he did. Gilliland, along with Bill McNew, disinterred the corpses and transported them to James Canyon near the northern edge of the Sacramento Mountains, where they were reburied.

The disappearance of Colonel Albert Jennings Fountain and his son baffled investigators for weeks. While numerous suspects were mentioned, clear evidence tying the abduction and presumed murder to anyone was lacking. It was whispered throughout the area that the law enforcement authorities investigating the disappearance were less than competent, that the Doña Ana sheriff's department was impotent as a result of lack of experience, politics, and cowardice. There were other whispers that most residents of the area were convinced Oliver Lee was involved with the crime, but that lawmen feared to confront him. After a time, the governor of New Mexico grew concerned that authorities were dragging their feet on the Fountain case and decided it was time to bring in some help.

Governor William T. Thornton was anxious for the Territory of New Mexico to qualify for statehood, but was concerned that the image of the state was one of lawlessness and ineffective law enforcement. The territory had not fully recovered from the headlines of years earlier related to outlaws such as Billy the Kid, Dave Rudabaugh, Jesse Evans, and others, as well as the horrors of the Lincoln County War. What the territory needed, believed Thornton, was a lawman with high visibility, with a track record of success, and one who could deal with, as well as charm, the public, the voters. Being a politician, Thornton settled on a man who had the potential to generate positive headlines, as well as a man who could generate similar publicity for Thornton. Even then, more than a century ago, politics was as much about publicity and show business as it is today. Thornton elected to recruit Pat Garrett.

PART III
THE ROAD TO ASSASSINATION

CHAPTER 17

THE CALL

As a result of losing the election for sheriff of Chaves County, as well as having to live with the fact that his former deputy, John Poe, backed another candidate, Garrett was angry and bitter. It was finally sinking in that the tide of public opinion which once regaled him as a hero, a fearless lawman, had shifted. His reputation had diminished considerably as a result of his failed business enterprises, his drunkenness, his belligerence, his indebtedness, and the perception of citizens that he was no longer effective. He decided it was time to leave New Mexico.

After disposing of his ranch and other holdings in 1892, Garrett and his family, now numbering eight children, along with Ash Upson, made the journey to Uvalde, Texas. Upson had been living with the Garretts in New Mexico.

Life for the Garretts in Uvalde was calm and peaceful when he was not drinking, but Garrett spent most of his time drinking with Upson. His main sources of income were gambling and racing horses. For the first time in years, Garrett had time to spend with his family, particularly his daughter Elizabeth, on whom he doted. Elizabeth was blind, and the rumors related to the blindness were not kind to the former lawman. One story that made the rounds held Garrett responsible for his daughter's handicap as a result of attacking her during a drunken rage and gouging out her eyes. Another rumor maintained that Elizabeth's blindness was the result of the wrong medicine administered to her when she was a baby. There exists no verification of either of these versions. The most commonly held explanation of the child's sightless condition was that she was born blind as a result of her father being infected with syphilis and transferring it to her mother. It was well known that Garrett entertained himself with prostitutes, and it was long suspected that he suffered from venereal disease. Like the other tales, this one is not supported by documentation. The truth is that Garrett proved to be a loving father to Elizabeth until the day he was assassinated.

After three years of racing and betting on horses in and around Uvalde, Garrett's losses exceeded his winnings, and he had to face the proposition that he was nearly broke again. He was considering leaving Uvalde and moving elsewhere to try to make a living. Before he could make a move, Ash Upson died on October 6, 1894. Garrett paid for the funeral and his friend was buried in the Uvalde cemetery. Following Upson's death, Garrett spent the next fifteen months trying to decide what to do, where to go. He was nearing his wit's end when in February 1896 he received the call to adventure in the form of a message from New Mexico governor William T. Thornton.

Colonel Albert Jennings Fountain, prominent soldier, politician, attorney, and newspaperman, along with his eight-year-old son Henry, had disappeared and efforts to locate them, or their bodies, had come to a standstill. Thornton believed it was time to bring in outside help, and Garrett was his choice.

It seems strange that Thornton would have selected Garrett, given the former lawman's decline in popularity. However Garrett was perceived, the fact remained that he still held the status of a celebrity by virtue of his claim that he killed Billy the Kid. Thornton was first and foremost a politician, and as such he sought headlines. Garrett was a guaranteed headline. Garrett decided to respond to the call.

The summons from Governor Thornton was Garrett's "Call." This type of summons, challenge, or invitation is what mythologist Joseph Campbell referred to as the Call to Adventure. With the Call, as writer Christopher Vogler explains it, "the seeds of change and growth are planted, and it takes only a little new energy to germinate them. The Call serves as a catalyst, a trigger to generate a new and different momentum on one's life."

The Call to Adventure can also carry with it an element of temptation. For Garrett, the temptation came in more than one form. First, there was the siren song of public office, of returning to a position of law enforcement. Such a position was often a catalyst for greater things, and Garrett had not completely given up his desire to be elected to some higher office.

Second, it is quite possible that Garrett was quick to respond to a challenge. Despite what others thought, Garrett, still an ego-driven man, perceived himself as a competent lawman, one capable of taking on a case and seeing it to a conclusion. From time to time over the years, Garrett had considered reentering law enforcement. Certainly, he missed the days when he was regarded as a hero, the man who finally put an end to the outlaw problems in Lincoln County. It is likely that Garrett missed the thrill of the chase.

Third, temptation can come in the form of, as writer Vogler says, "the glint of gold." Garrett was deeply in debt with limited to near-nonexistent sources of income. What money he did come up with more often than not went for alcohol, gambling, and prostitutes. The "glint of gold" offered by Governor Thornton could be the cure for many of his problems, and it is likely that was the particular temptation that Garrett succumbed to the most. According to documentation in the possession of his son, Jarvis Garrett, the former Lincoln County sheriff estimated that the job of tracking down the kidnappers of Albert Fountain and his son was worth at least $15,000, a significant amount of money in those days.

Garrett was ready for the Call. He was fed up with the way his life was going, and he sought new horizons, different challenges, and other adventures. The disappearance of Colonel Albert Jennings Fountain provided the opportunity. More than willing, Garrett responded positively and made plans to return to New Mexico. As he set out on his journey, little did he realize that he had set himself on the road to assassination.

Governor Thornton invited Garrett to meet with him in February in El Paso, Texas. Garrett was already planning to be in town to watch the fight between future heavyweight champion Bob Fitzsimmons and Peter Maher, which was then postponed. Garrett and Thornton visited in the governor's hotel room. Following a long discussion on a variety of topics including statehood, the Doña Ana County sheriff's office, and the disappearance of Colonel Fountain, the meeting ended and Thornton returned to the capital at Santa Fe. Within a few days of returning, Thornton filed a recommendation that Garrett be appointed chief deputy and given total jurisdiction in the Fountain case. He recommended Garrett receive a salary of $500 per month plus expenses. The recommendation was not without opposition.

CHAPTER 18

RETURN

WHILE PAT GARRETT WAS GONE FROM NEW MEXICO, THE office of sheriff of Doña Ana County had become embroiled in area politics, more so than ever. Both Albert Fall and Albert Fountain regarded the office of Doña Ana County sheriff a vitally important one because the person in charge of that station was in a position to protect and assist elected politicians. During the election for sheriff of 1894, Fall supported the candidacy of Guadalupe Ascarate. Fountain backed the Republican opposition, Numa Reymond.

By the time the polls closed for lunch on election day, eighty-eight votes had been cast. After voting got underway after lunch, someone discovered the morning ballot box was missing. It was later found in the post office. Ballots were still in the box, but it was obvious that they had been tampered with—every one of them had been marked Democrat. For reasons unexplained, no one moved to void the election. It was decided to continue with the afternoon voting and discuss the controversy at a later time. At the end of the day when the afternoon votes were counted, it was found that the majority of them had been cast for Reymond. In order to determine whether or not the tampered with morning votes should be counted, the commissioner's court went into session. As their discussion got underway, Oliver Lee, wearing a

US deputy marshal's badge, walked into the room to observe the proceedings. Lee was sporting a revolver in a holster on his hip. Most researchers agree that the presence of Lee, a known killer of men and a man to be feared, intimidated the court members into accepting the controversial morning ballots. By the time the meeting was adjourned, Fall's candidate Ascarate was declared the winner. Incensed, Fountain filed an appeal on behalf of Reymond, one that was still pending when he disappeared. In addition, a lawsuit against the county was filed.

After taking possession of the sheriff's office, Ascarate learned of Governor Thornton's recommendation to appoint Pat Garrett as a Doña Ana County "chief deputy." On hearing the news, Ascarate expressed anger. He stated that he resented the intrusion into the operations of his office, and he insisted he was not inclined to allow others to determine who his deputies would be, not even the governor.

Numa Reymond reentered the picture and, likely as a result of a consultation with Fountain, announced to the Democrats that if Ascarate resigned and allowed Garrett to be named sheriff that he would drop his appeal and lawsuit. The most strenuous objection to this proposal came from Albert Fall.

It was a bizarre and uncomfortable situation Pat Garrett was about to stumble into, and ultimately become a part of.

On February 24, Garrett was invited to another meeting in El Paso. In addition to Garrett and Governor Thornton, according to the *Rio Grande Republican*, some of "the most prominent men in New Mexico" were in attendance. Thornton chaired the meeting. Speaking for all present, he invited Garrett to pursue the Fountain case as a private detective. He was to be paid $8,000 if he succeeded in obtaining an arrest and conviction, plus $150 per month for expenses. He was also promised an opportunity to be considered for the office of sheriff.

Garrett accepted the offer with no hesitation. The offer was timely, for he was broke, again. The position would help in fulfilling his ego, but was also an important financial decision. Not long after accepting the offer, Garrett moved his family back to Las Cruces. In 1900, he sold his Uvalde farm to close acquaintance and future vice president John Nance Garner.

Garrett never returned to Uvalde. In Las Cruces, he focused on his new mission —to solve the Fountain case. He was also eager to return to politics.

Garrett's return to law enforcement proved to be much more difficult than he could have imagined. Only a few days into the job as an investigator, Garrett began to feel the frustration of not being able to make decisions about the Fountain investigation. Instead of being in charge of the case as he had been led to believe he would be, Garrett discovered he had been provided with no authority to make arrests, nor was he allowed to enlist the assistance of citizens. Garrett was not used to being a subordinate.

Garrett was further angered to learn that he was not to be appointed sheriff of Doña Ana County. It soon became clear to him that the entire territory of New Mexico—the governor, the press, and the citizenry—were watching him and waiting for him to make his next move. When little to no investigative momentum had been gained relative to the Fountain case, severe criticism of Garrett soon followed. Some of the harshest denunciations came from Elfego Baca, a Socorro lawman.

Like Pat Garrett, Elfego Baca possessed a huge ego. He wanted to be a famous lawman, and once stated that he wanted "the outlaws to hear my steps a block away." When Sheriff Baca obtained a warrant for the arrest of a lawbreaker, instead of pursuing the wanted man he would send him a letter that stated: "I have a warrant for your arrest. Please come in by [date] and give yourself up. If you don't, I'll know you intend to resist arrest and I will feel justified in shooting you on sight when I come after you." In addition to being a lawman, Baca enjoyed careers as a lawyer and politician.

Baca loudly asserted that Governor Thornton had picked the wrong man to lead the Fountain investigation. It was reported that Baca also claimed he knew more about the Fountain abduction and presumed murder than anyone else in New Mexico, and that only he was capable of identifying and arresting the killers.

Governor Thornton was stung by Baca's proclamations but, knowing of the lawman's propensity for boisterousness, chose to ignore him. Outwardly, Garrett made it clear that he paid no attention to Baca's statements and feigned a lack of concern about the matter. Given the growing criticism, however, Garrett was aware that he needed to demonstrate some progress with regard to the Fountain case, thus he decided to assume some focus on the matter.

Garrett had received information from a variety of sources that claimed Oliver Lee was behind the kidnapping and likely murder of Colonel Fountain and his son, and undertook an effort to have Lee arrested. Other sources suggested Fountain was alive and well and had decided to flee the country. One rumor had him escaping to the West Coast with a mistress. Rumors spread that he had been spotted in other cities as well as in other countries. The source of most of the rumors was Albert B. Fall, all of which were printed in his newspaper, the *Independent Democrat*.

Governor Thornton began to convey some misgivings about Garrett's appointment and expressed concerns that the lawman might never experience any success. In spite of what Thornton regarded as a shrewd political move in naming the man who was credited with killing Billy the Kid to take charge of the investigation, he was also aware of Garrett's character issues. As a result, Thornton contacted the Pinkerton Detective Agency and requested assistance.

The Pinkertons had been organized by Allan Pinkerton, a former bodyguard to the late President Abraham Lincoln. By this time, the agency had been in operation for almost five decades and had experienced successes and generated headlines by assisting in the solutions to labor disputes and serving as strikebreakers. On occasion, the Pinkertons were known to resort to violence to achieve results, including beatings and shootings.

Thornton contacted the Denver office of the Pinkerton agency, which was headed by James McParland. McParland, in turn, assigned agent J. C. Fraser to apply his detective skills to assisting in the Fountain investigation. Fraser arrived in Las Cruces on March 10, 1986, much to the surprise and dismay of Pat Garrett.

When Fraser arrived at the sheriff's office, which served as a base of operations for investigator Garrett, the tension and animosity between the two men were palpable. Fraser, who was a highly trained and skilled detective and had the reputation of being able to get along with any and all, found it difficult to break through Garrett's hostility toward him. In contrast to Fraser, Garrett was untrained and chafed at the distinction. His enormous ego balked at what he considered an intrusion into his realm as chief investigator. Garrett was further perturbed when he learned that Governor Thornton requested progress reports on the Fountain case from Fraser and not from him.

Fraser never stopped trying to get along with Garrett, but was rebuffed at every turn. Garrett refused to share information with the Pinkerton man. In his reports to the governor, Fraser never wrote anything negative about Garrett, but it was obvious he was becoming frustrated by his antagonism and unwillingness to cooperate.

After reviewing the available evidence, Fraser recommended initiating indictments for the arrests of Oliver Lee, James Gilliland, William McNew, and Bill Carr. As a consulting detective, Fraser had no authority to initiate warrants or make arrests.

Fraser also wanted to have Albert B. Fall arrested as an accomplice, but eventually realized that proving complicity against the elusive and scheming politician would be an uphill battle. Garrett informed Fraser that arresting Lee et al. was a bad idea because of the political landscape of the time and place, and recommended that such action be delayed until he was named sheriff. He also told Fraser that he was convinced they needed more evidence. Fraser argued that he had developed an impressively strong case for the arrest and prosecution of the suspects and that all it needed was for Garrett to obtain statements from them. Fraser was concerned that all Garrett knew about the case was what he had learned from Fountain supporters and told him so. Garrett, who did not like to be criticized, was taken aback by the rebuke.

Garrett tried to convince Fraser that arresting Lee and his companions would be difficult, that they would not be easy to find, that they were dangerous, and that they would lie. Garrett argued for developing a case against Lee and his men slowly and carefully. He also suggested that they identify someone close to Lee who might be willing to provide evidence, and suggested either Gilliland or McNew as prime candidates to turn.

In the meantime, Albert Fall decided to work his cunning and wile on Garrett. Fall, ever the scheming politician, decided Garrett could be useful to him. Fall was convinced that Garrett would eventually be named Doña Ana County sheriff and he wanted to make certain that the lawman believed that Fall was a man to have on his side. Fall decided to provide the appearance that he and Garrett could be friends.

On March 15, Fraser called on Garrett at his hotel room and found him deep in conference with Fall. Garrett told Fraser that Fall wanted him to be named deputy sheriff and that Fall would make himself available to assist in any manner whatsoever. Fall had told Garrett that he would undertake a lobbying effort in Santa Fe in favor of the position. Garrett later told Fraser that if he were not named deputy sheriff that he would resign from the case. Fraser expressed concern that if Garrett did not receive the appointment and departed, there would be no one left to initiate the necessary warrants against Lee and the others. It was clear to Fraser that those currently in charge of the Doña Ana County sheriff's office would be unwilling to make the arrests out of fear. Fraser decided to report this predicament to Thornton.

While Thornton was pondering options, Fraser went around Las Cruces soliciting some support from prominent businessmen to weigh in on the matter with local judges and others in authority. His efforts paid off: On March 19, District Judge Gideon Bantz declared Numa Reymond the winner of the previously disputed election. The following day, Ascarate moved out of the sheriff's office and Reymond moved in. Fraser believed that the situation was now right for Garrett to be provided with a greater level of authority.

Garrett made an appointment with Reymond and wasted no time in asking him when he was going to name him chief deputy as well as the date in the near future when the entire office of the sheriff would be turned over to him. To Garrett's surprise, as well as Fraser's, Reymond informed him that he had no intention of appointing him chief deputy or of turning over his office to him. Reymond then told Garrett that he had appointed Oscar Lohman to the position of chief deputy, and that the best he could do for Garrett was to hire him as a regular deputy and that he would thus take orders from him, Reymond. In a rage, Garrett stormed out of the office and reported the results of the meeting to Fraser.

Since Reymond's stance was not conducive to furthering the Fountain investigation, Fraser decided to attempt another strategy. He met with Major W. H. H. Llewellyn of the state militia and requested a favor. Llewellyn agreed, and met with a number of Las Cruces businessmen. The fruits of his effort yielded $1,000 that was to be used to bribe Lohman. Within days after receiving the money, Lohman announced that he was no longer interested in the position of chief deputy. Several days later, Garrett was appointed to the position. Though evidence for such has not been found, it is believed by many that even more money was raised and passed along to Reymond, for in the last week of April the sheriff suddenly submitted his resignation. When all was said and done, Pat Garrett was named the new sheriff of Doña Ana County in March of 1896.

During this period of political manipulation and the efforts to win the office of sheriff for Garrett, precious little time or energy was applied to investigating the Fountain case. The only effort manifested was that attributed to Pinkerton agent Fraser.

Once Garrett was finally ensconced in the office of sheriff, he took stock of the situation. All of his life he had been a staunch Democrat, but he now found himself obligated to Republicans for his present position. And if he aligned himself with the Republican Party, he was taking a chance of suffering defeat at the next election. Loyalty to the Democratic Party was now in competition with practicality, as well as Garrett's pride and self-image. He decided, therefore, to abandon the Democratic Party. (At the next election, he ran as an independent and won. Shortly after his victory, Garrett announced that he was now affiliated with the Republican Party.)

Any advances made relative to the Fountain investigation during the political squabbles in the sheriff's department were being accomplished by Fraser. During his inquiries, he encountered a man named Slick Miller who was serving time in a New Mexico prison for cattle rustling. Miller had been sentenced to prison by Albert Jennings Fountain. Under questioning, Miller revealed that back in 1894, plans were made by Oliver Lee, Bill McNew, and Bill Carr to kill Fountain. Miller claimed that the man in charge of the plot was named Ed Brown, a small-time cattle rustler from Socorro and a close acquaintance of Lee's. Before the assassination could be carried out, however, Fountain's efforts at breaking up the area cattle rustling operations had succeeded in inhibiting Brown's plans.

A Pinkerton agent named S. B. Sayers decided to approach Ed Brown with an offer of immunity if he would provide information leading to the arrests and convictions of the Fountain killers. Before doing that, however, Sayers decided he wanted to frighten Brown.

Brown was tracked down and subsequently arrested. He was formally charged with cattle rustling, a crime he denied. Sayers, in the company of local law enforcement officials, attempted to intimidate Brown into believing that if he did not give up relevant information pertaining to the Fountain case, he could expect to spend a long time in prison. Brown did not respond as the agent and lawmen expected him to. He was not to be cowed by the lawmen; he denied any knowledge of a plot to kill Fountain, refused to provide any information of any kind, and eventually had to be released.

Deciding that the time and energy invested by its operatives in the Fountain case was yielding little in the way of progress, the Pinkerton Detective Agency decided to call its agents home. Fraser and Sayers were pulled out on May 16, 1898. The sole remaining investigator in the case was Pat Garrett.

CHAPTER 19
CHASING OLIVER LEE

WITH PAT GARRETT FINALLY SETTLED INTO THE OFFICE OF Doña Ana County sheriff, he began to acquire a new and different set of problems. While the newspaper headlines about the Fountain disappearance remained ubiquitous, and while Garrett devoted some bit of time and energy to the case, he found that much of his day was taken up with the mundane duties associated with enforcing the law in the county. In addition to the normal responsibilities of the sheriff, in July 1896 Garrett was awarded the post of US deputy marshal. The reason for this assignment was related to the growing number of immigrant Chinese laborers being smuggled into the United States from Mexico. For years, hundreds of Chinese had been employed as laborers during the construction of over one thousand miles of railway throughout Mexico. With most of that work completed, and faced with constant discrimination and even violence, the Asian workers began to perceive that greater opportunities for employment, as well as a better quality of life, lay north of the border. Garrett's federal appointment was connected to facilitating the investigation of migrant activity in his jurisdiction. In addition, Garrett, who always seemed to be broke, needed the money.

Two years had passed since the disappearance of Colonel Fountain and his son, Henry. Garrett, who did more idling than investigating, was no closer to solving the case than when he started. Governor Thornton's term ended and Miguel Otero was elected to the position. Otero was not impressed with Garrett's progress, or lack of such, with the Fountain investigation, and he insisted on some pertinent action by and results from the sheriff. Goaded by Otero's demands, Garrett made some moves to seek indictments. A number of Doña Ana County citizens were convinced that Garrett was dragging his feet in filing charges against Oliver Lee and his crowd because he feared the rancher. It was long past time for Garrett to demonstrate that he was active on the case.

The grand jury was set to meet on April 1, 1898, to review the charge against Lee. Garrett traveled to Tularosa to serve notice on prospective jurors. While in town, Garrett entered Tipton's Saloon and encountered Oliver Lee, Albert Fall, District Clerk George Curry, and owner Tobe Tipton playing poker. When Tipton left the game to attend to business, Garrett took his seat. What followed was a seventy-hour card game, with Garrett and Lee prodding each other. The game became tense. Observers noted that both men were armed, and that neither of the two were inclined to turn their back on the other.

During the game, Lee informed Garrett that if he intended to serve papers on him, he knew where he could find him. Garrett replied that if that were the case he would send them to him or have them delivered by Curry. When the game finally broke up, Garrett rode back to Las Cruces.

On the morning of April 2, Garrett approached Judge Frank Parker and requested bench warrants for the arrests of Oliver Lee, Jim Gilliland, Bill McNew, and Bill Carr. In his deposition, Garrett stated that the aforementioned men were the ones who killed

Colonel Fountain and his son, in spite of the fact that no bodies were ever found. Garrett's deposition was supported by Major W. H. H. Llewellyn and Thomas Brannigan, who stated that they found evidence indicating that the Fountains had been murdered. The following day, Garrett arrested McNew and Carr. Both men were so surprised that they offered no resistance. They were placed in the Las Cruces jail and held without bond.

Garrett didn't seem quite as enthusiastic about arresting Oliver Lee. While in Las Cruces, Lee learned of the arrests of McNew and Carr. He returned to his ranch without encountering the sheriff. He had no sooner entered his ranch house when a posse of ten deputies reined up in front. It appeared as though Garrett preferred to have a contingent of deputies confront and arrest Lee rather than take on the job himself. Lee stood on the porch and glared at the riders, then turned and stepped inside.

Clearly, the members of the posse were also intimidated by Lee, a man known to be fearless and to have killed others. One of them suggested that they enter the house and place the rancher under arrest, but the majority were in favor of abandoning the task and returning to Las Cruces. As the men debated their next move, Tom Tucker, a Lee ranch hand, stepped out onto the porch, faced the posse members, and told them that Lee was not at home. Unsure of themselves and confused about what to do next, the deputies turned their mounts and rode back to Las Cruces. Later that day, Lee arrived in El Paso. While there, he was interviewed by a newspaper reporter who inquired about the warrant for his arrest. Lee told him that he had no intentions of allowing himself to be placed in the custody of Pat Garrett.

Lee was convinced that Garrett did not have enough evidence to convict him of anything. Lee was surely aware that he intimidated the sheriff, and that Garrett knew that he was well connected politically. Whatever Garrett felt about Lee, he continued to drag his heels with regard to the Fountain investigation and was suffering the increasing displeasure of Governor Otero, as well as a growing number of citizens.

Lee was more concerned that his cowhands McNew and Carr, who were in jail, would tell Garrett more than Lee wanted him to know. Lee was also concerned that Garrett might offer either or both of the prisoners a deal wherein they would be set free if they provided enough information to convict the rancher. It turned into a waiting game.

Albert Fall learned that McNew and Carr were in custody and figured Garrett was leaning on them. Despite his patronization of the sheriff, Fall was much closer to Lee when it came to politics and power. Based on recent investigations by western cold case detective Steve Sederwall, it is also likely that Fall was complicit in the disappearance and murder of his archenemy, Albert Jennings Fountain. If Lee were taken down for the crime by Fountain, Fall might soon follow. Fall undertook efforts to have McNew and Carr released from jail as soon as possible. Within a few days, he managed to schedule a preliminary hearing for the two men. Fall's strategy was related to the notion that if they were to remain in jail, the prosecution would be forced to show its evidence, and Fall and Lee were desperate to know what they had.

The grand jury hearing got underway during the first week of April 1898. A man named Jack Maxwell was introduced and seated in the witness chair. Garrett had intended for Maxwell to be his star witness, a decision that later turned out to be a poor one. Maxwell testified that he was at Lee's ranch house on the day that Fountain disappeared. He stated that Lee, Gilliland, and McNew were not present but arrived much later on trail-weary horses. Maxwell stated that the three men appeared to be deeply concerned about something.

During his testimony, Maxwell was nervous and unsure of himself. Fall sensed his discomfort and, like a shark going after a wounded fish, attacked him. Fall was too much for the inarticulate and unconfident ranch hand, and Maxwell crumpled under the onslaught. During questioning, Maxwell admitted that Garrett had agreed to pay him $2,000 if his testimony would send Lee, Gilliland, and McNew to prison. Fall implied that Garrett had bribed the witness to provide testimony that would be useful to Garrett, true or not.

By the time Fall finished with the now frightened Maxwell, the cowhand had done more damage to Garrett and the prosecution than to Lee and his companions. The hearing continued for six days. Garrett, who should have known better, paraded one useless witness after another before the court. None of them provided anything in the way of evidence or pertinent testimony, only opinions.

While Garrett was wasting everyone's time at the hearing, it was learned that all of the evidence gathered at the site of the presumed Fountain abduction and elsewhere along the pursuit route had mysteriously vanished.

By the time the hearing wound down, the judge ordered Carr released from jail but declared that McNew must remain without bond. Garrett found something in this decision to bolster his flagging spirits, for he was convinced that McNew would eventually yield to pressure to gain release. In this, Garrett also erred. McNew remained under arrest for almost a year, and during that time he provided not a scintilla of useful testimony.

CHAPTER 20

CONFRONTATION

As the investigation into the Fountain case muddled along, it became clear that Garrett and Oliver Lee were destined to confront one another again. It was to occur weeks later, an exchange of gunfire would be involved, and once again Garrett would slink away badly defeated and embarrassed.

Garrett's star was continuing to dim, and he was aware of it. Whatever prestige he once enjoyed had long since faded. People have short memories, and their recollections of the days of Billy the Kid's rustling adventures and the subsequent pursuit by Garrett, if they had any at all, were now a generation old. Further, Garrett's inability to make any progress on the Fountain case left the impression among many that he was little more than a political appointee and lacked investigative competence. Spending much of his time trying to advance his cause with politicians and moneyed businessmen, Garrett had little to do with the average citizen of Doña Ana County, and most of them had nothing to do with the sheriff. Months had passed since the swearing out of indictments for Lee and Gilliland, and the two men were still at large. The consensus among New Mexicans was that Garrett was afraid of tangling with Lee.

Garrett knew that he needed to do something to change the momentum, as well as to change the perceptions of the voting public. He sought an opportunity to reposition himself in the eyes of the populace. One such chance to do so was on the horizon, one that would have put to rest all of the concerns about his abilities as a law enforcement officer. It would turn out to be another opportunity, however, that he somehow managed to bungle.

Garrett knew that he had to eventually face Lee. The rancher, along with Jim Gilliland, continued to elude the incompetent sheriff at every turn. The two fugitives rarely went near Lee's Dog Canyon ranch house, for it was suspected that it was under surveillance. It was rumored that they had grown beards and ranged throughout southern New Mexico. On one occasion, the two men passed near a Garrett posse, but no one recognized them. On another occasion, Garrett and Oliver Lee passed each other on a road. Lee was sporting several days' growth of beard and was wearing old, worn out clothes, appearing as a down and out cowhand. Garrett did not, or appeared not, to recognize the fugitive. Ranchers W. W. Cox and Print Rhode, both of them brothers-in-law to Lee, provided the two men with supplies, a place to hide, and fresh horses when needed.

On the afternoon of July 1, 1898, two members of Garrett's posse—Clint Llewellyn and José Espalin—rode up to a corral in the foothills of the Organ Mountains where they spotted Lee and Gilliland working cattle. The four men, all of whom knew each other, spent several minutes in conversation. During the visit, Lee mentioned that he and Gilliland were preparing to ride to Wildy Well, a nearby location on Lee's property, where they would spend the night at the cabin. Before riding away, Espalin warned Lee to be careful and that Garrett was on the hunt and not far away. After leaving Lee, the two deputies rode straight to Garrett and told him about Lee's plans.

Garrett, now aware of Lee's location, decided it was time to confront the rancher and place him under arrest. He wasted no time in assembling a posse, which consisted of José Espalin, Clint

Llewellyn, Kent Kearney, and Ben Williams. Kearney seemed an odd choice for a posse member; he was a schoolteacher who possessed no experience whatsoever with law enforcement or firearms.

Garrett led the posse on the trail toward Wildy Well just before sunset, intending to cover the forty miles during the dark of night. By 4:00 a.m., the lawmen were within one mile of Wildy Well where they reined up, tied off their horses, and continued on foot toward the cabin.

The dwelling was a small house constructed of adobe with an attached wagon port. The roof of the port was a few feet lower than that of the house. Nearby were a pump house, a water tank, a corral, and scattered outbuildings. In the corral, Garrett spotted horses belonging to Lee and Gilliland. Garrett led his men toward the house.

With revolver in hand, Garrett stepped up onto the porch and put his ear to the door. He heard snoring coming from inside. He tried the door latch and found it unlocked. Garrett indicated to Kearney, who was standing nearby, that he wanted the deputy to accompany him into the structure. A second later, Garrett pushed the door open, stepped inside, jammed the tip of his weapon into the first sleeping person he encountered, and shouted that they were all under arrest.

The focus of Garrett's attention turned out to be neither of his quarries, but Mary Madison, who rose to a seated position in the bed and screamed. She, her husband, James, their two children, and a man named McVey were all sleeping in the cabin. The Madisons were in Lee's employ as caretakers of the Wildy Well portion of his ranch. All were awakened and confused. Garrett herded them outside and demanded to know where Lee and Gilliland were but received no response. He decided he would have to go search for them.

As Garrett and his deputies searched the outbuildings, the sheriff glanced back toward the cabin and spotted McVey attempting to communicate with someone on the roof. Typical of such dwellings, the roof was flat, with the adobe walls of the structure projecting two feet above the level to form a parapet. Garrett realized immediately that it could serve as a substantial defensive position. Grabbing a ladder, the sheriff carried it to the cabin and leaned it against one wall. He instructed McVey to climb the ladder and inform the men on the roof that they were under arrest and to surrender immediately. McVey refused. Garrett turned to James Madison and repeated the order. Madison also refused.

Garrett then ordered Deputy Williams to take a position behind the water tank, then instructed Llewellyn to move the Madisons back into the house and stand guard over them. He, Espalin, and Kearney moved the ladder over to the wagon port and the three climbed to its roof. From where they stood, they could see a portion of the cabin roof but saw no one there. One of the deputies secured a smaller ladder that was lifted to the top of the port and leaned against the wall of the house. Kearney climbed a couple of rungs up the ladder to get a better view. At the same time, according to Garrett, he yelled for whoever was on the roof to surrender. On the ladder, Kearney was in a position to look onto the roof where he saw one or more of the men who had been sleeping there. Kearney fired his revolver, and at the same time, Garrett sent several shots from his rifle onto the roof. During a subsequent interview, Lee said this was not true, that the call for surrender came only after Garrett and his deputies began shooting.

Lee stated he "was asleep when fired upon," though it is difficult to believe that he and his companions remained asleep with all of the activity taking place below in the house and yard, as well as the screaming of Mary Madison. Further, it has been observed that McVey had been talking to someone on the roof. Lee said, "Kearney fired twice, and Garrett also fired before I fired.

I heard no commands of 'hands-up,' but Garrett was talking while shooting."

It was later learned that four men had been sleeping on the roof: Lee, Gilliland, and two of Lee's ranch hands, one of whom was Todd Bailey. As far as can be determined, this was the first time Garrett had encountered Bailey; it would not be the last.

Two of Garrett's bullets struck the roof close to Lee, scattering gravel, dirt, and twigs. Lee fired back. One of the ranch hands also fired, the bullet striking Kearney in the shoulder and shattering bone. He fell from the ladder, rolled across the wagon port roof, and slammed hard down onto the ground.

Feeling exposed, Garrett jumped from the port roof and, ignoring the severely wounded Kearney, raced for shelter inside one of the outbuildings. Espalin lowered himself from the roof, but rifle fire from Lee and his men confined him to a position against one wall of the cabin. Several bullets tore holes in the water tank under which Deputy Williams was hiding. Cold water spilled onto the helpless lawman. Unable to flee, he was forced to remain under the dripping tank. This left Garrett as the only member of the posse who was in a position to continue the fight.

According to R. L. Madison, who was a boy at the time of the gunfight, Lee called Garrett a bastard and scorned him for shooting at men at the same time he was calling for them to surrender. Garrett yelled for Lee to lay down his arms and give up, but the rancher refused, stating that he was convinced that Garrett was going to kill him if he did.

According to Buck Bailey, the grandson of Todd Bailey, Lee ordered the lawmen to drop their guns. Garrett replied that he was afraid to because he feared Lee would kill them. Lee told Garrett that he was a man of his word and that if he and the deputies laid down their weapons he would let them ride away. Garrett finally agreed.

As Garrett was leaving, he passed by Kearney and saw that he was badly wounded, in severe pain, and might not live. From the roof of the cabin, Lee repeated his order for the lawmen to ride away. Author Leon Metz refers to this as "the most humiliating episode of Garrett's life." Despite the element of surprise that Garrett believed he had carried into the Wildy Well fray, he and his posse had been forced to surrender, leave their weapons, and ride away. Much to Garrett's discredit, he chose to leave the badly wounded Kearney behind.

The lawmen rode a few miles to a location known as Turquoise Siding where they encountered a railroad section line crew. Garrett convinced some of the men to take a wagon to Wildy Well and retrieve Kearney. When the railroad workers arrived later, they found Kearney being attended to by Lee and his cowhands. Kearney was transported to Turquoise Siding where he was loaded onto a train and taken to Alamogordo. There, he was placed in another wagon and carried to La Luz. He died the following day.

Garrett and his deputies returned to Las Cruces. His mission to arrest Lee and Gilliland was a failure, and the two fugitives were still at large.

CHAPTER 21
POLITICAL MACHINATIONS

Two years had passed since Pat Garrett had been brought on board as the chief investigator in the disappearance and likely murder of Colonel Albert Jennings Fountain and his son, Henry. Save for the arrest of Bill McNew, nothing had been accomplished. Even having McNew in custody proved to be inconsequential for he had provided nothing significant in the way of incriminating evidence against Oliver Lee and Jim Gilliland. Governor Otero was growing ever more impatient with Garrett, as were the citizens of New Mexico. In the meantime, Garrett continued to collect a monthly paycheck while making it appear to the voters that he was indeed active in the investigation.

Not only were Lee and Gilliland wanted in relation to the Fountain case, they now faced an additional charge for the murder of Kent Kearney. (It was never determined which of the men on the roof of Lee's cabin at the Wildy Well ranch fired the shot that killed Kearney.) Most area residents were convinced that Lee and Gilliland refused to surrender to Garrett because they were convinced their safety could not be guaranteed, that Garrett wanted them dead. As Lee and Gilliland were on the run from Garrett, Albert B. Fall returned to Las Cruces from a stint in the US Army. He wasted no time at all in jumping into the fray and insisted that arrangements be made to guarantee the safety of his two clients.

To compound the difficulties faced by Lee, rumors spread throughout the Tularosa Basin that Jim Gilliland, always a boastful sort, was bragging to acquaintances about his role in the killing of Fountain and his son. Fall was concerned that Gilliland was talking too much, and that if he was arrested by Garrett, that he might reveal too much information.

Fall considered a number of strategies. He knew for certain that Lee and Gilliland could avoid the inept Sheriff Garrett for as long as they needed to, but that chase needed to come to an end eventually. He pondered the notion of having the fugitives surrender to law enforcement authorities outside of Garrett's jurisdiction, a move that he realized stood the greatest chance of success. Fall considered Garrett untrustworthy and did not wish to turn his clients over to him. Fall had what he thought was a brilliant idea: He would have Lee and Gilliland submit to authorities in a different county. He decided that it would enhance their chances, and his prestige as a lawyer, if he could arrange to have a new county formed, one that encompassed the site of the Fountain abduction.

Fall met with W. A. Hawkins, an attorney for the El Paso and Northeastern (EP & NE) Railroad. Hawkins had earlier proposed the formation of a new county for a different reason. The EP & NE Railroad had purchased a significant portion of Oliver Lee's Dog Canyon Ranch in 1897 in order to construct a system of canals across it to deliver water from the Sacramento Mountains to railroad stations along the line. At the time, Lee's property was located in Doña Ana County, but, to Hawkins's frustration, county officials were less than helpful to the railroad company. County roads, if they existed at all, were poorly maintained, and the bureaucrats appeared reluctant to address the situation. Hawkins therefore lobbied for a new county, with the county seat to be located in Alamogordo. Albert Fall volunteered to assume the responsibility for petitioning for a new county as long as it was agreed that the western boundary would extend to the San Andres Mountains, thus incorporating the White Sands where the Fountains disappeared, and therefore assuming legal jurisdiction. Doña Ana County, where Garrett was sheriff, would be removed from all legal responsibility.

The plan for the new county was in place. Now, Fall found it necessary to convince the state politicos that it was a sound idea. He encountered resistance immediately from Thomas Catron, a prominent Republican senator in the territorial legislature. Catron did not care for Fall, a Democrat, and voiced his disapproval of the plan at the outset. Governor Otero, who also harbored a dislike for Fall, opposed the idea. Furthermore, both Catron and Otero were convinced that Oliver Lee was behind the Fountain killings and they were not inclined to do anything that would make his arrest and prosecution more difficult.

A close examination of the historical progress made relative to the formation of the new county reveals that W. A. Hawkins and Albert Fall were considerably more intelligent and cleverer than the two politicians, Catron and Otero. Knowing well that moves and decisions made by politicians were often, if not mostly, strongly determined by ego, they proposed that the new county be named after the governor. Within hours of having this idea presented to him, Governor Otero reversed his position and decided it would be a good idea, in fact, to have a new county. Otero's primary opposition to the idea was Catron, whose own ego was likely bruised by this plan. Catron acquiesced, however, when it was agreed that Fall would be supportive of Catron's own proposal to establish a new county in the western part of the territory to be named after President McKinley.

Agreements were made, and Otero County became official on January 30, 1899. Within a few weeks, George Curry was elected sheriff. Plans got underway to deliver Oliver Lee and Jim Gilliland to law enforcement authorities in the new county, thus avoiding Pat Garrett.

CHAPTER 22

CONFRONTATION REDUX

WHILE ALBERT FALL AND W. A. HAWKINS WERE BUSY FACILI-tating the formation of Otero County, Oliver Lee had traveled to and was living in San Antonio, Texas. There he married Winnie Rhode, a sister-in-law of W. W. Cox, one of Lee's neighboring ranchers. The two men were close, and the union of the Lee and Cox families was to eventually impact Pat Garrett.

By March 1899, Lee and Gilliland had returned to New Mexico and were living at the home of Eugene Manlove Rhodes in the foothills of the San Andres Mountains. Rhodes was a diminutive man with a severe speech impediment. Years later, he became a noted author of books about southwestern ranches and ranchers. He was also known to provide sanctuary for men on the run and had harbored a handful of wanted outlaws over the years, including the noted train robber, Black Jack Ketchum.

Rhodes was sympathetic to the plight of Oliver Lee and Jim Gilliland. At the same time, he was an admirer of Pat Garrett. Rhodes began positioning himself to make arrangements for the surrender of Lee and Gilliland to Sheriff Curry of the new Otero County. There were two conditions: The two men would not be placed in the Doña Ana County jail, and they would not be handed over to Sheriff Pat Garrett.

On being apprised of this plan, Sheriff Curry contacted Governor Otero and requested advice. Otero agreed that the conditions could be met. Working together, Rhodes and Curry arranged to have the two fugitives taken to Las Cruces, surrender to Judge Frank Parker, and then be delivered to the jail at Alamogordo, the new Otero County seat. On March 13, 1899, Lee and Gilliland, both wearing minimal disguises and accompanied by Rhodes, boarded a train at Socorro and headed for Las Cruces. Unknown to Rhodes, Lee, and Gilliland, Pat Garrett was aboard the train. Garrett, along with Texas Ranger Captain John Hughes, was transporting a prisoner from Santa Fe to El Paso.

According to Rhodes, Garrett and Hughes entered the smoking car where Lee and Gilliland were seated. For several minutes, Hughes thumbed through a magazine as he stood next to the seat occupied by Gilliland. Garrett made his way down the aisle and stopped next to the seat occupied by Oliver Lee. Garrett bent down and stared past Lee and out the window at the passing countryside. Several minutes passed, and the two lawmen, neither of them lingering long enough to enjoy a smoke, turned and walked away.

According to writer W. H. Hutchinson, there is little agreement among historians as to whether or not the two lawmen recognized Lee and Gilliland. Gilliland, however, was convinced that they did, and implied that Garrett was too frightened of Oliver Lee to make an arrest, or even say anything. Gilliland was likely correct in his assessment. It is difficult to believe that Garrett was fooled by the blue eyeglasses worn by Gilliland and the beard worn by Lee. Garrett was an experienced lawman, and he had been close to both men on several occasions. Garrett had sat opposite Oliver Lee during the seventy-hour poker game at Tipton's Saloon in Tularosa only a few months earlier.

When the train arrived at Las Cruces, Rhodes escorted Lee and Gilliland to the home of Judge Parker, where the two men formally surrendered. As it turned out, the jail at Alamogordo was still under construction and unable to accommodate prisoners. As a result, Lee and Gilliland were installed in the Las Cruces jail in spite of the earlier agreement not to do so. A few days later, Parker agreed to have Lee and Gilliland placed under the authority of Socorro County sheriff C. F. Blackington and placed in the Socorro jail. Days later when construction on the Otero County jail was completed, Blackington escorted the prisoners to El Paso where they were loaded onto an EP & NE train and delivered to Alamogordo. There, Lee and Gilliland were placed in the new jail. As the two prisoners conferred with their lawyer Fall and awaited their trial for the murder of Albert Jennings Fountain and his son, logistical difficulties arose.

CHAPTER 23
COX RANCH KILLING

As LEE AND GILLILAND WAITED IN THE ALAMOGORDO JAIL, PAT Garrett was well on his way to further antagonizing men who were already growing weary of him and his presence in New Mexico, men who would eventually factor into decisions about whether the sheriff would live or die.

Garrett received a telegram from Sheriff George Blalock of Greer County, Oklahoma, that a man named Norman Newman, alias Billy Reed, was wanted for murder and was known to be living on the ranch of W. W. Cox. On October 7, 1899, a warrant was issued for Newman's arrest. Garrett, accompanied by Sheriff Blalock, traveled to the Cox Ranch in a buckboard. Deputy José Espalin followed on horseback. Garrett was aware that Cox was not at the ranch; he was away on business. His wife, who was several months pregnant, was home.

William Webb Cox, originally from Texas, had a youth speckled with hardship and violence. His father, James W. Cox, held an office with the state police, an agency installed by the Reconstruction government and largely despised by the Texas citizenry for their bullying and often violent tactics. The elder Cox was killed during an ambush by a mob of Karnes County citizens led by the noted outlaw, John Wesley Hardin. Young W. W. Cox chanced by the ambush scene several hours later and found his

W. W. Cox

RICHARD KOLB

father's body riddled with fifty-eight bullet wounds. Cox swore revenge and took it. He was arrested, found guilty, and sent to prison for several years. Cox escaped, gathered up his family, and fled. He arrived in Doña Ana County, New Mexico, in 1890. He began acquiring land and placing herds of cattle and horses on it. In time, Cox became a successful and respected rancher, and eventually owned and operated one of the largest spreads in the area.

Cox was an able stockman and was respected and admired by his ranch hands. He always wore a starched white shirt, a string tic, and a vest, even when working cattle. He smoked hand-rolled cigarettes from the time he woke up in the morning until he went to bed at night. Cox rarely spoke a sentence that wasn't laced with profane words. Cox and Oliver Lee became brothers-in-law, and in spite of that relationship he got along well with Pat Garrett, or at least appeared to, even lending him money on occasion.

As Garrett, Espalin, and Blalock arrived near the Cox ranch house, they decided to park the buckboard and proceed the rest of the way on foot, leaving Blalock behind to tend to the horses. Garrett and Espalin made their way to a position behind the house, crossed the backyard, and stepped up to the open kitchen door where they spotted a man inside washing dishes. Pointing a revolver at him, Garrett asked him if he was Billy Reed. When the man replied that he was, Garrett told him he was under arrest.

In spite of the fact that he was face-to-face with a wanted murderer, Garrett inexplicably holstered his weapon. One second later, Newman slammed a punch into Garrett's face. Stunned, Garrett pulled the handcuffs from his belt and swung them at Newman, cracking them across his head and knocking him to the ground. Both Garrett and Espalin fell atop Newman and attempted to cuff him. At the same time, a bulldog charged in from an adjacent room and attacked the newcomers. The bulldog, oddly, belonged to Albert B. Fall. Newman fought with the lawmen while they tried to fend off the bulldog. Newman finally broke free and ran outside toward the smokehouse. He knew that Cox kept a spare revolver in the outbuilding and he was intent on retrieving it. Newman was standing in the open doorway of the smokehouse when two gunshots sounded, one of the bullets striking him in the back and tearing through his heart. He died instantly. Garrett and Espalin entered the smokehouse and pulled Newman's body out, dragged it to the buckboard, placed it in the wagon bed, and returned to Las Cruces. During the subsequent inquest, Espalin admitted he fired the shot that killed Newman.

When W. W. Cox returned to his ranch several days later and learned what had transpired, he grew angry. He was particularly incensed that his pregnant wife had been subjected to the violence and terror. Cox never said anything to Garrett about the incident, however, and not long afterward lent the perpetually broke sheriff some more money.

While Cox appeared to have taken Garrett's intrusion into his home in stride, the same could not be said for his wife's brother, Print Rhode. When Rhode learned of the incident and the stress it had caused his sister, he was outraged. Rhode swore he would kill Garrett.

Print Rhode was a short, muscular cowhand who seldom went out of his way to avoid confrontation. Regarded as an adept cowman, Rhode was also good at fighting. He had arrived in New Mexico with Cox and had become one of his most trusted ranch hands.

Garrett had very few friends he could count on. It appeared he was more adept at making enemies. Cox and Rhode, brothers-in-law to Oliver Lee, represented two more adversaries that would give the sheriff reason to keep looking over his shoulder.

CHAPTER 24
THE TRIAL OF OLIVER LEE

As Albert B. Fall made preparations to defend Oliver Lee and Jim Gilliland in court, he was convinced that it would be impossible to assemble a fair and impartial jury in Otero County. The prosecution pressed to have the trial held in Las Cruces, but Fall effectively argued that since that was Fountain's hometown, most of the jury would be prejudiced. A compromise was finally reached: The trial would be held in Sierra County in the tiny mining town of Hillsboro.

The process commenced on May 25, 1899. Hillsboro, the county seat, boasted one hotel, a schoolhouse, a sheriff's office, a jail, and a smelter. There was no telegraph and no railroad. A stagecoach came through town once a week. Hillsboro was a relatively isolated community, and most of the town's residents were unaware of the disappearance of Colonel Fountain and the efforts of Pat Garrett to arrest the suspects.

When the time and location of the trial were announced, friends and families of the accused, along with selected witnesses, began arriving. Since there was not much in the way of accommodations, most camped in the surrounding foothills. Soon, the curious were showing up, as well as newspaper reporters, until the crowd swelled into the hundreds in a town too tiny to accommodate them.

Senator Thomas Catron was appointed special counsel for the prosecution by Governor Otero. Catron believed that if Lee and Gilliland were found guilty, it would be viewed as a victory for the Republicans, and as such would enhance the prestige of Catron as well as that of Sheriff Pat Garrett. If Lee and Gilliland were found not guilty, it would be viewed as a victory for the Democrats as well as a major setback for the Republicans. Albert B. Fall, the attorney for the defense, was determined to rout the Republicans and continue the momentum toward his longed-for rise to power.

Jury selection took place May 25 through May 27. Several of the jurors selected were Mexican-American residents of Hillsboro and had little facility with the English language. As a result, an interpreter was brought in to translate as the trial went along.

At the outset, Fall charmed the onlookers. He was approachable, stopping to speak with any and all residents and visitors as well as newspapermen, shaking hands and slapping backs. When speaking to them, Fall characterized the trial as a contest between the working class, represented by ranchers and farmers and miners just scraping by, working from dawn to dusk, against the wealthy, the major landowners, and the elite. Fall carefully constructed for himself the image of a giant killer, and explained that his enemy was an evil power that wielded a heavy hand over the region. Such words resonated with the area residents.

By contrast, the name Catron was synonymous with political corruption. Unlike the blue-collar multitudes in Hillsboro, Catron was a soft, portly bureaucrat who likely never experienced hard work of any kind in his life, a man perceived by the lower classes as making his living by arranging for taxes on the working masses.

Pat Garrett, despite his lingering prominence, was associated closely with the establishment Republicans and was largely ignored. By contrast, when Lee and Gilliland arrived at Hillsboro they were surrounded by well-wishers and treated as celebrities.

Thomas B. Catron
RICHARD KOLB

Like Fall, they mingled with the citizenry, shaking hands and smiling.

When the trial opened, Lee and Gilliland were formally charged only with the murder of Henry Fountain. Charges related to the deaths of Albert Fountain and Kent Kearney were held back to be filed at a later date. The prosecution rationalized that the disappearance and presumed killing of an innocent youth would generate sympathy among the jurors. If Lee and Gilliland could be convicted of the death of Henry Fountain, then the subsequent trials related to the deaths of Albert Jennings Fountain and Kent Kearney would stand an excellent chance of conviction.

At the outset of the trial, however, the prosecution began to grow concerned. Key witnesses failed to show up. The apparent sympathies of the general Hillsboro population and the new arrivals for Lee and Gilliland, along with the clearly manifested dislike of Catron and his allies, was troubling. On May 29, the trial got underway.

Todd Bailey, along with two other Lee ranch hands, had accompanied Lee and Gilliland to Hillsboro. Bailey sat near the front of the courtroom and to one side. Another Lee ranch hand sat on the other side, and a third sat in the back. Each of the cowhands carried concealed weapons, including a shotgun, rolled up in his saddle slicker.

As the trial opened and progressed, things began to go poorly for the prosecution. Catron, along with his associate counsel, was no match for the wily Albert Fall. Fall was aggressive and relentless, and it was clear that the jury grew excited when he questioned witnesses. The prosecution was less energetic, less dynamic, and its performance paled next to that of Fall.

When Pat Garrett was called to the stand, he and Fall engaged in a back-and-forth that was judged to end in a tie. In the end, however, Garrett, in spite of his prolonged investigation into the Fountain case, proved to be not particularly helpful to the prosecution.

The trial plodded on, and after a few days both prosecution and defense rested. Before hearing the final arguments, a short break was called. A half-hour later, the courtroom was called to order and each side prepared for the arguments. Todd Bailey and the other two Lee cowhands took up their previous positions in the courtroom. Hidden beneath the folds of Bailey's saddle slicker was a modified shotgun. Earlier in the day, Bailey shortened the barrel and the stock of the weapon in order for it to be easily concealed. The other two cowhands were similarly armed. Years later, Todd Bailey explained his role at the trial. He stated that if Oliver Lee were found guilty, he and the other two ranch hands would rise up, pull their weapons, and kill Garrett, the other deputies in the courtroom, along with the prosecuting attorney. Following this, according to a plan that been developed during the previous days, they would escort Lee out of the building and ride to a location outside of town where more of Lee's men were waiting with horses. From there, the entire group would travel for several miles, with a pair of cowhands splitting off from time to time to confuse any trackers. Lee and Bailey would continue on to Mexico.

The prosecution enlisted Richmond P. Barnes to deliver the final arguments. It proved to be a poor decision. Barnes regarded himself as a skilled orator, an opinion held only by him. He quoted from Charles Dickens's *Pickwick Papers*, which only confused the jurors who looked at one another in bewilderment. The Mexican Americans understood little to nothing of what Barnes was saying and likely had no acquaintance with Dickens's literary works. Translation was provided by the court-appointed interpreter, but it turned out that he had no more of an idea of what Barnes was trying to say than anyone else.

When the long-winded Barnes finally finished, the prosecution then sent William B. Childers in to attempt to repair some of the damage. His arguments merely muddled an already confused prosecution. Childers rambled on, and by the time he had finished, it was well into the evening. In spite of the late hours, it was now time to hear the arguments for the defense. Albert Fall rose and faced the jurors, several of whom appeared to be falling asleep. Fall hoped to rouse them with his presentation.

The jurors, seeing Fall standing before them, were now fully alert and gave the attorney their full attention when he called the Doña Ana County officials "broken down political hacks . . . gathered together as does the slimy filth at the edges of a dark eddy." He told the jurors, most of whom were poor residents of Hillsboro, that the Territory of New Mexico spent a great deal of money, money from their taxes, to prosecute the accused, but that the defendants, all salt-of-the-earth working men like themselves, were forced to pay for their defense out of their own pockets.

Fall pointed out that no bodies had ever been found, and stated that based on the evidence presented by the prosecution, "you would not hang a yellow dog." When Fall turned and indicated that he was finished, the entire courtroom, excluding the prosecution, burst into loud applause that lasted for several minutes.

When the applause died down, Tom Catron, who was not well liked among the Hillsboro citizens, rose for a rebuttal. Like Barnes and Childers, Catron had little talent for reading the jurors, and he discoursed for two-and-a-half grueling hours. It is doubtful that many of the jurors heard much of what Catron had to say. They, like many of the spectators, had fallen asleep. By now they were desperate to be excused.

It was not to be. Albert Fall rose and moved that the jury adjourn and render a decision before retiring for the night. Fall knew well that the jurors now had a strong dislike for all of the members of the prosecution, and he did not want to allow them time to get over it. It was 11:30 p.m. when the jury was escorted back to their meeting room. Several of the spectators left for their beds, but many remained, convinced a decision would not be long in coming. It took the jury all of eight minutes to arrive at a verdict. When they were called back in, Todd Bailey and his companions checked their weapons and readied themselves for the final decision.

With Lee and Gilliland, along with Fall, standing and prepared to receive the judgment, the jury foreman rose, and with no preliminaries whatsoever, announced the verdict: not guilty.

The crowd in the courthouse broke out into applause and cheering, and the celebration lasted for more than an hour. The members of the prosecution team, along with Pat Garrett, slunk out of the courtroom and, a short time later, out of town. Realizing what they were up against with Fall, they elected not to pursue the charges against Lee and Gilliland for the murders of Colonel Fountain and Kent Kearney.

The decision was a severe blow to Pat Garrett, both professionally and personally. He had invested three years of his time in bringing the suspects into a courtroom, only to see them turned loose. His investigation was regarded by most as unimpressive, even incompetent, and in the end yielded nothing.

Garrett was embarrassed, and he was smart enough to realize that his days as a lawman in the Territory of New Mexico were coming to an end. Desperate, he began to cast about for some other line of work that would pay enough for him to continue to pursue his vices.

During the previous three years of pursuing the mystery of the Fountain disappearance, Garrett had made a formidable enemy in the form of Oliver Lee. Lee was not a man to forget, and in the coming months, the rancher watched Pat Garrett as the hawk regards a mouse.

CHAPTER 25
COLLECTOR OF CUSTOMS

WITH THE TRIAL OF OLIVER LEE OVER AND HIS REPUTATION AS a competent lawman in tatters, Pat Garrett entered another phase of transition; he was heading toward a career crossroads. His days of being in the spotlight and hobnobbing with the political and social elite were eroding. Garrett was regarded as a man of few social graces, his personality tending toward the abrasive, and he had acquired the reputation of a drunkard and a failed gambler. More and more Garrett was excluded from community affairs and other events of Doña Ana County.

Some things remained constant for Garrett—his unabated problem with alcohol and other vices, along with his indebtedness. He owed money to a number of people and saw little opportunity to make enough to pay them back. In time, he realized he would not be able to remain in that part of New Mexico much longer, so he cast about for other opportunities. He set his sights on El Paso, Texas.

During the previous few years, El Paso had experienced significant growth and prosperity, and business opportunities abounded. A great deal of El Paso's business came from Juarez just across the border, and as a result thriving import-export businesses evolved. Much of the US-bound traffic from Mexico involved great herds of cattle driven from the interior ranges and purchased by ranchers in Texas and New Mexico. Near the border in downtown El Paso stood a customs house. The government-established operation oversaw the trade of goods coming from Mexico, and the Customs District of El Paso del Norte encompassed all of Texas as well as Arizona and New Mexico Territories. The collector of customs here supervised nine hundred miles of international border and was paid $2,000 per year, an impressive salary for the time. It was to this position that Pat Garrett directed his attention.

With support from a few friends, Garrett petitioned President William McKinley. He was confident it was just a matter of time before the president rewarded him with an appointment to the position. Unfortunately for Garrett, McKinley was assassinated a few months later and succeeded by Theodore Roosevelt. Roosevelt, as it turned out, was not impressed with the current collector of customs in the El Paso district, H. M. Dillon. Roosevelt wanted a proven leader, a man unafraid to tackle the many difficult issues that faced the customs office, and a Republican. Oddly, Garrett convinced his old enemy Albert Fall and former New Mexico governor Lew Wallace to submit letters of recommendation to Roosevelt and, this done, made arrangements to travel to Washington, DC, to meet with the president himself. His efforts were successful, and Garrett was nominated for the position of collector of customs on December 16, 1901.

The nomination was forwarded to the US Senate for approval, and Garrett was invited for an interview. During the meeting, which was attended by a number of politicos, the subject of his gambling came up, but Garrett, ever the liar, denied any involvement in such. Garrett was confirmed on December 20, 1901.

Garrett returned to El Paso and moved into his new job. As author Metz states, it was not long before Garrett's "grating personality" began to create problems. In addition, Garrett managed to add to his list of enemies, among them influential politicians and businessmen. Disputes arose over Garrett's evaluation of cattle coming across the border, and before long a petition calling for his dismissal was being circulated, and a number of complaints began arriving at the desk of his superior in Washington, Secretary of the Treasury Leslie M. Shaw. Shaw sent a reprimand to Garrett, who responded by sending an angry letter to President Roosevelt. Roosevelt was now growing concerned with what was turning out to be a controversial appointment, but was too occupied with other more important matters to take any action and deferred to Shaw.

Treasury Secretary Shaw sent an agent named Joseph Evans to El Paso to evaluate Garrett's performance. Evans advised Garrett to remove himself from the cattle inspection duties and appoint George M. Gaither to the position. Garrett refused, but under pressure from Evans finally did so on March 9, 1902. Garrett and Gaither did not get along right from the start, and on May 8, the two men got into an argument on a busy El Paso street that evolved into a fistfight witnessed by two-dozen onlookers. Both men were arrested, charged with disturbing the peace, and fined $5 each. The report of the incident reached Shaw's desk one week later, and another reprimand was sent to Garrett. Shaw was growing weary of Pat Garrett.

In 1905, Garrett decided it would enhance his career if he attended the Rough Riders convention in San Antonio, an event directed by Roosevelt. Tom Powers, one of Garrett's gambling friends and the owner of El Paso's Coney Island Saloon, convinced the customs inspector to take him along. Garrett told Powers that he was to identify himself as a cattleman, since hanging around with a known gambler would not go over well with the president. Garrett introduced Powers to Roosevelt and the three men posed for photographs, one of which appeared in a local newspaper. Roosevelt subsequently learned that Powers was not a cattleman, but a gambler, and was convinced that he had been duped by Garrett. Caught in the lie, the politically inept Garrett made plans to travel to Washington and take Powers with him. He reasoned that if the president got to know Powers he would come to like and admire him. Roosevelt refused the meeting, and on December 13, 1905, he informed Garrett that he would not be reappointed as collector of customs.

CHAPTER 26
FINANCIAL DIFFICULTIES

AFTER LOSING HIS JOB AS COLLECTOR OF CUSTOMS, PAT GAR-
rett returned to his ranch on the eastern slope of New Mexico's
San Andres Mountains, a ranch he purchased in 1898. Because
Garrett was disgraced, historians have wondered why he would
return to Doña Ana County where his list of political and other
enemies had grown significantly. The truth was, Garrett had no
place else to go.

Garrett's ranch was a good one: He had plenty of water, and
he stocked his range with beef and dairy cattle, as well as horses.
For a time, Garrett supplied beef to a Las Cruces butcher and
sold milk to the families of the miners living not far away at
Gold Camp and Oro Grande. Most of Garrett's attention, however, was devoted to his horses, which he continued to enter in
races throughout New Mexico, West Texas, and Mexico. Garrett
enlisted his teenage son, Poe, to serve as a jockey.

Garrett's horses soon became a concern for his neighbors.
Because fencing was inadequate to nonexistent in the area, his
long, slim-legged racehorses bred for speed and not for work had
wandered onto the pastures of ranchers who desired tough, working animals. Mixing their mares with Garrett's studs produced
an offspring that was useless for ranch work. More enemies were
added to Garrett's list, and these new ones included his neighbors.

In May 1899, Garrett had acquired Bear Canyon in the San Andres range, a parcel of land adjoining his ranch and seven miles from his house. The Bear Canyon land had a small cabin, a corral, and a spring of cool, clear water. Garrett was interested in the mineral potential of the Bear Canyon property and initiated a survey. While there was little promise of a rich deposit of the silver, gold, and other minerals found in the area, Garrett decided more money could be made from selling mining interests. With W. H. H. and Clint Llewellyn, the Alabama Gold and Copper Mining Company was formed, with Garrett serving as secretary of the corporation. The stated objective of the company was to acquire and operate gold and silver mines in the area, but it was a lie. The three men did nothing at all related to prospecting and mining ore. Instead, they issued worthless stock for sale. The company disbanded two years later.

It occurred to Garrett that the only person who made any money during the mine investment business was the lawyer who assisted them. It occurred to Garrett that the lawyers he knew—Albert Fall, Thomas Catron, others—all lived well and appeared to have a lot of money. Garrett decided to become a lawyer.

With no education or experience whatsoever, Garrett paid a small amount of money in Mexico and obtained a license to practice law. Unfortunately for him, the license was only good in Mexico and he was unable to practice in the United States. A short time later he was hired to defend a man charged with murder. As a result of Garrett's inexperience and lack of knowledge, he lost the case. His client was sentenced to a life term in a Mexican prison. Coming to grips with the notion that his future did not lie in the practice of law, Garrett returned to his ranch in Doña Ana County. There, life was becoming even more difficult for him.

Garrett learned on his return that, as a result of a bill that had remained unpaid for months, he no longer had credit at the grocery store where he and his family purchased provisions and supplies. In the weeks and months following, Garrett found himself in court over his debts. Each of the banks in the area had notes on Garrett and none had any success in collecting. Garrett still owed Thomas Catron $500 he had borrowed years earlier; he had not repaid a penny on the debt, in spite of several letters from Catron. With the banks and businessmen forming up against Garrett, he acquired the reputation of a deadbeat in and around Doña Ana County.

During January of 1898, the Second Judicial District Court declared that the Albuquerque Bank of Commerce had the right to collect from Garrett the full sum that was owed, along with interest, court costs, and attorney costs, plus damages amounting to another $1,000. The court provided for the seizure of Garrett's property, and ordered Doña Ana probate clerk José R. Lucero to carry out the order. Lucero returned the paperwork with the explanation that Garrett did not own any land, that two men held legal notes on his ranch. One of them was W. W. Cox, Oliver Lee's brother-in-law.

The other man who held a note on Garrett's ranch was Martin Lohman, from whom Garrett had borrowed over $3,500. The note included Garrett's ranch, houses, improvements, thirty head of cattle, and 150 head of horses. The note required Garrett to pay Lohman the money within one year. Convinced he could turn the money into a greater fortune, Garrett decided to use it for gambling, but as usual he lost more than he won. After two years of receiving no payments on the loan from Garrett, Lohman sold the note to W. W. Cox for $2,000. Like Lohman, Cox was unsuccessful in getting Garrett to pay anything on the note. Cox considered seizing Garrett's property but instead decided to extend the note for an additional year.

More judgments were filed against Garrett. On learning that Cox and Lohman held notes on Garrett's property, the Albuquerque Bank of Commerce scheduled meetings with a judge and convinced him that the bank held the first rights to Garrett's ranches based on an 1898 claim against him, one that predated any of the subsequent mortgages. The court ruled in the bank's favor. On May 14, 1906, José Lucero was given the authority by the New Mexico Supreme Court to seize Garrett's ranches, all buildings, and all livestock, and place them up for sale at auction.

When W. W. Cox learned of the state's intention to seize Garrett's property, he gathered a few ranch hands and rode to the ex-lawman's ranch. There, Cox and his men rounded up all of the cattle they could find and herded them over to his ranch. He informed Garrett that he was seizing the cattle and would keep them until he paid what was owed. When Lucero arrived at Garrett's ranch, he could locate only a few cattle that Cox had overlooked.

An appraisal was made of Garrett's property. The 160 acres, including buildings and corrals, were valued at an astonishingly low $225. His spring, on the other hand, was valued at $250, perhaps an indication of how important and valuable water resources were in this part of the country during this time. The appraisal did not include the Bear Canyon part of the ranch. During the subsequent auction, the Albuquerque Bank of Commerce outbid all others and took ownership of the Garrett properties for $1,000. According to the laws of the time, Garrett was given one year to repay all of his debts before he would be forced to vacate his property. Though no details have been located, Garrett was somehow able to accommodate the bank and remain on his ranch for the remainder of his life. That, however, was not destined to be very long.

Just as Garrett was beginning to think that most of his problems were coming to an end, a new one surfaced. Though Garrett had resided on his ranch for six years, he had never paid any taxes. An official from Doña Ana County notified him that he owed $922.72. Garrett was informed that if he did not pay this amount by August 1906, the county would seize his stock and auction it off to satisfy his tax obligations. Nearly all of Garrett's stock, however, had been relocated on the ranch of W. W. Cox.

Because Garrett owed Cox a lot of money, the rancher informed him he was not going to return any of the animals. On August 17, Cox pressured Garrett to sign a bill of sale for the entire herd of cattle for "one dollar and other valuable considerations." When Lucero, who by this time had been elected sheriff of Doña Ana County, arrived at the ranch, he seized everything Garrett owned, including personal possessions, and sold the entire amount at auction for only $6.50. Garrett was allowed to keep his horses.

CHAPTER 27
WAYNE BRAZEL

PAT GARRETT'S LIFE WAS PERPETUALLY ON A DOWNHILL SLIDE that appeared to be gaining momentum, and was destined to get worse. Never an easy man to get along with, Garrett now found himself with very few friends and growing troubles. He owed money to prominent people and institutions throughout the area, and his abrasive personality, often fueled with alcohol, helped matters not at all. During the previous few months he had gone from being mildly disliked to being completely despised. The few times he came into town he was, as Metz described, "quarrelsome and insulting, brawling drunkenly in the streets." Garrett threatened people and provoked fistfights. The bigger and more experienced ex-lawman was frequently victorious, but of late he was more often than not thrashed by smaller, sober opponents.

Garrett particularly hated rancher W. W. Cox, and seethed at the notion that Cox maintained control of his herd of cattle until the debt was paid off. Garrett argued that without the cattle he was unable to make any money, but Cox was unsympathetic. Garrett's rage against Cox grew by the day. Garrett gathered up his family and moved to Las Cruces in hopes of encountering opportunities to make some money. Finding nothing there, he left his family and moved to El Paso where he landed a job: He was hired to sell real estate.

Not long after arriving in El Paso, Garrett moved in with a woman identified only as "Mrs. Brown," a known prostitute. The two were often seen dining and drinking together and riding around town in a buggy. It was never learned how much real estate Garrett sold, if any, but it was clear that he was spending a great deal of money on liquor.

Before leaving his ranch, Garrett turned over the duties of running it to his son Poe. In Garrett's absence, and without consulting him, Poe signed an agreement on March 11, 1907, with an area cowhand named Jesse Wayne Brazel, to lease the Bear Canyon ranch for five years.

Brazel was to figure prominently in the life of Pat Garrett over the next eleven-and-a-half months he had left to live. Born in Kansas in 1876, Brazel's family moved soon afterward to Lincoln County, New Mexico, and then to Gold Camp, the small mining community near Garrett's ranch. As a youngster, Brazel found work on Cox's ranch and impressed everyone with his commitment and performance. Cox was so fond of Brazel and so appreciative of his hard work and loyalty that many in the area thought the two men were related. Brazel saw Cox as a mentor and an inspiration.

In time, Brazel cast about for additional ways to make more money than he was earning as a common cowhand. While still working for Cox, he also landed a job as a swamper at a Las Cruces saloon. Following some discussions, Brazel and Print Rhode, Cox's brother-in-law, decided that some good money could be made raising goats. Cattlemen cared little for goats, claiming that they competed with cattle for grass, often ruining pastures. On the other hand, goats were low-maintenance and high-profit livestock. Brazel and Rhodes looked around for a suitable pasture for a goat herd, and decided that Garrett's Bear Canyon ranch was the best place to locate their animals.

Wayne Brazel
RICHARD KOLB

The biggest obstacle to obtaining the Bear Canyon ranch for Brazel and Rhode was Garrett himself. Garrett and Rhode despised one another, a hostility that stemmed from the earlier fight with, and killing of, Norman Newman at the Cox ranch. Rhode was also aware that Garrett hated goats. Knowing that Garrett was away in El Paso and that son Poe was managing the ranch, Brazel approached him to work out details of the lease. Because Poe was aware of the hatred Garrett held for Rhode, the partner's name was never mentioned. Brazel also withheld the information that they planned on installing goats on the ranch, for all were also well aware of Garrett's hatred of them. The terms of the lease called for the payment of ten heifer calves and one filly colt, leaving the impression that that was the type of livestock that was to be placed on the property.

During July and August of 1907, Brazel and Rhode began stocking the Bear Canyon property with goats. When Poe learned of this, he contacted his father in El Paso. A man of quick temper, the enraged Garrett raced back to the ranch to put an end to the lease and drive the goats off his land. On arriving, he learned that Brazel was in partnership with his enemy Rhode. Given Garrett's style, some researchers assumed Garrett's plan was to bully Brazel off the property, but given the alliance with Rhode he had second thoughts. It is believed by many that Garrett feared Rhode, a tough and violent man. Further, when Garrett learned that the goat-raising operation had been subsidized by another enemy, W. W. Cox, he grew livid.

Garrett decided to take the matter into the courtroom and filed a complaint with Organ, New Mexico, justice of the peace Charles M. Anthony. Since Organ had no courthouse, the hearing was held in the town's butcher shop. As the town's citizens filed into the shop to watch the proceedings, Rhode taunted Garrett and challenged him to a fistfight, but the latter backed down.

It turned out to be impossible to assemble an impartial jury in Organ, and Anthony refused to serve as an arbitrator. He knew that whatever decision was made would antagonize at least half the town. He decided to call a recess for several months in the hope that tempers would cool and a solution would be arrived at.

Desperate for money, Garrett wrote a letter to George Curry requesting a loan. Garrett already owed Curry money that he had borrowed from him over the years, and the governor, though he realized it was not likely that he would ever be repaid, still sent Garrett a check in return mail.

CHAPTER 28
CHINESE LABORERS

DURING THE LATE 1800S AND EARLY 1900S, HUNDREDS OF MILES of railroad were constructed throughout Mexico, most of it by using imported Chinese laborers. The Asians arrived in Mexico with promises of steady work at decent pay. Though the work was steady—twelve to fourteen hours per day, seven days a week—the pay was dismal, and the Chinese families lived in poverty.

By the time the Mexican Revolution was winding down, most of the railroads had been built and hundreds of Chinese now found themselves out of work. As a result of discrimination and lack of employment, life for them in Mexico was unbearable, so they set their sights north of the border and undertook a migration in that direction. At the time, however, the United States was not welcoming to Chinese immigrants and refused them access. The Chinese Exclusion Act that placed a moratorium on Chinese labor was passed in 1882. Between that year and 1920, however, it has been estimated seventeen thousand Chinese entered the United States to fill vacant jobs.

A number of the Asians crossed the border illegally, most of them transported by contractors who were hired to provide laborers for railroad construction, the mines, and farms and ranches in southern Colorado. Hundreds had crossed in this manner, and a staging area was sought where they could remain until the time arrived for them to move on to Colorado. The demand for labor in Colorado was great, with thousands of jobs waiting. The person, or agency, that could provide such help stood to make a great deal of money from smuggling and transporting available laborers, and the Chinese represented an important commodity to them. The temptation to make significant money by smuggling illegal Chinese attracted a group of men in southern New Mexico. They included Oliver Lee, W. W. Cox, Print Rhode, Carl Adamson, Mannen Clements, and Jim Miller.

Mannen Clements was serving as a constable in El Paso during much of the time he was associated with Oliver Lee and company. As constable, Clements busied himself with shaking down prostitutes and bullying most of whom he came in contact with. Clements was described as an unsavory character. A cousin of outlaw John Wesley Hardin and the father-in-law of Jim Miller, Clements was a known cattle rustler and killer of men, and worked as a sometime gun for hire.

Texan Jim Miller led a varied life holding down jobs as a ranch hand, a deputy sheriff, and a Texas Ranger. As a lawman, Miller was known to have a penchant for killing Mexicans whether they were guilty of anything or not. Despite these immoral and unsavory activities, Miller regarded himself as a devout Christian and an avid churchgoer and was never known to drink or curse. He was often referred to as Deacon Jim Miller. After moving to Fort Worth, Texas, in 1900, Miller advertised himself as a professional assassin. He charged $150 for each killing. His first victim was his brother-in-law, and since then it had been estimated that he had assassinated at least forty men. His weapon of choice was a shotgun. He was thereafter known as Killin' Jim Miller.

While Garrett was dealing with the Bear Canyon difficulties, the sinister element in the form of Killin' Jim Miller arrived in El Paso, a man who, like Oliver Lee, W. W. Cox, Wayne Brazel, Print

Mannen Clements
RICHARD KOLB

Rhode and others, was to figure heavily into the life of Garrett. Miller had strong connections with several of Garrett's enemies.

Carl Adamson was a brother-in-law to Miller. Adamson had been involved in a number of dealings with Oliver Lee in the past, and was knowledgeable, and likely very active, in the smuggling of illegal Chinese laborers. The word was planted in the area that Miller and Adamson had a herd of over one thousand cattle in Mexico and wanted to move it to a ranch in Oklahoma. They

Killin' Jim Miller
RICHARD KOLB

made certain that the word reached Pat Garrett. Before getting their stock across the border, as the story went, they needed to find a location where they could fatten the cattle up before the long journey. The two men arranged to have a meeting with Garrett to discuss the possibility of using his Bear Canyon ranch. The truth was that Adamson and Miller had no cattle. They wanted the location to hide the smuggled Chinese.

Information related to the smuggling operation came to light from Dr. W. C. Field (sometimes spelled *Fields*). One day, Field was called to treat a man for some undisclosed ailment. On arriving, Field saw that his patient was Chinese, a man who had been smuggled across the border at El Paso and was currently residing in the county jail at Las Cruces. As he was being treated, the man revealed to Dr. Field the smuggling arrangements and named many who were involved. On returning to his office, Field wrote a letter containing this information to US Marshal Creighton Foraker, who in turn passed it on to other federal agents. Following this, US marshal and Secret Service agent Fred Fornoff was sent to the area to investigate. Much of what follows is derived from Fornoff's investigation reports.

As numbers of Chinese were smuggled across the Mexican border at El Paso and some New Mexico locations, the smugglers were in need of a remote and safe place to hold them until such time as they could transport them north into Colorado. Garrett's Bear Canyon Ranch was considered ideal for this purpose. For this plan to work, it was necessary to get Brazel's goats off of the ranch. Lee, Cox, and others decided on a plan. Enlisting Carl Adamson and Jim Miller, it was agreed that the two men would approach Garrett about leasing his Bear Canyon Ranch to hold a herd of over one thousand head of cattle they intended to bring up from Mexico. They offered Garrett top dollar for the use of his ranch to fatten the cattle up until such time as they could move the herd to Oklahoma. They never mentioned a word about the illegal Chinese to Garrett.

The potential arrangement held a strong appeal for Garrett. He saw a chance to make some easy money by leasing the Bear Canyon property. He told Miller and Adamson that he was willing to make a deal but that the property was currently leased to a goat herder. Garrett explained that if he could arrange to have the lease broken and the goats moved elsewhere, then it would be an easy matter of stocking the cattle on it. Miller arranged for a meeting with Brazel.

Brazel refused to cancel the lease, but made an exception if he were paid $3.50 for each goat in his herd. He told Garrett and Miller that he had twelve hundred goats on the land. Miller agreed, a lawyer was summoned, and a contract drawn up.

Later, in a meeting with Garrett, Miller offered him $3,000 for the Bear Canyon property. If he would agree to the terms, Miller told him, he and Adamson would also hire him to drive the cattle from Mexico to the Bear Canyon location and oversee them until such time as they could be shipped to Oklahoma.

Anticipating the pending lease of the Bear Canyon property along with the herding arrangement, Garrett was reveling in what he perceived as his newfound good fortune. He quit his job at the real estate firm, returned to Las Cruces, and moved his family back to the ranch. Garrett, who seemed to be followed by bad luck wherever he went, was unprepared for the difficulties that were soon to follow.

Within a few days after returning to his ranch, Garrett was notified by Brazel that he had miscounted the number of goats on the Bear Canyon property, and that instead of the figure of twelve hundred he quoted earlier, he now insisted that he had eighteen hundred animals. Brazel told Garrett that if he paid him for the entire herd, he would withdraw from the lease. On being informed of these new conditions, Jim Miller told Garrett that the agreement they made would have to be cancelled. Garrett pleaded, but Miller held firm.

Just when he thought he had the promise of a brighter future in his grasp, Pat Garrett's life instead proceeded along its familiar downward spiral. Desperate again for money, he wired Governor Curry and asked for a $50 loan.

It was clear to Lee and his partners in the venture that Garrett would eventually figure out that no cattle were forthcoming. It is believed that, knowing well that Garrett was deep in debt, they considered offering the ex-lawman a piece of the action. The main problem with this strategy was that Lee and Garrett were sworn enemies and hated one another. In addition, Garrett had grown very uncomfortable around W. W. Cox and Print Rhode, and was perhaps in fear of both men.

Lee had learned through experience not to trust Garrett. Lee suspected that if Garrett were invited to participate in the smuggling plot, he would not only refuse, but was likely to alert law enforcement officials. In this manner, Garrett could exact a certain amount of revenge against men who tormented him in the past, some of whom he owed a lot of money.

Lee knew that Garrett had mentioned to others that he was still interested in pursuing the killings of Albert Fountain and his son, Henry. Further, Garrett was now the principal obstacle to the Chinese smuggling operation. To Oliver Lee, there was only one clear solution to these problems: Pat Garrett had to go.

CHAPTER 29
RAILROAD TIES

WHILE OLIVER LEE WAS PONDERING WHAT TO DO WITH PAT Garrett, a unique business opportunity presented itself, one that had the potential to make a great deal of money. For years, there was talk of running a railroad line from El Paso, Texas, to Alamogordo, New Mexico, and eventually all the way up to Chicago. The first official attempt came in 1895 with the El Paso, St. Louis, and Chicago Railway and Telegraph Company undertaking the planning and construction. It was known as the El Paso and Northeastern Railway. When the line to Alamogordo was completed, little time was lost in the building of a branch line stretching from Alamogordo to the pine and fir forests of the Sacramento Mountains to the east. The main purpose of this new line, called the Alamogordo and Sacramento Mountain (A&SM) Railway and which extended into Cloudcroft in 1900, was to haul logs harvested from the forests back down to an Alamogordo sawmill, which converted them into railroad ties that were necessary for the continued construction of the railway northward.

Recognizing a grand opportunity, a cabal of confederates organized a company to supply railroad ties to the EP & NE Railroad. It is unclear who came up with the idea, but the company consisted of Oliver Lee, Albert B. Fall, W. H. H. Llewellyn, Llewellyn's son Morton, George Curry, and W. A. Hawkins, a former law partner of Fall's and at the time an attorney for the EP & NE Railway.

After being cut, the logs were loaded onto A&SM Railroad flatcars and hauled into Alamogordo where they were transferred to a sawmill and transformed into the railroad ties that were sold to the EP & NE Railroad. While the timber harvesting company made impressive profits, the truth was that all of its activities were illegal. For one thing, it is believed by many that most, if not all, of the timber cutting was accomplished with illegal Chinese laborers brought to the site by Oliver Lee and his partners. For another, the logs were harvested from federal land without permission.

When, after a period of time, it became clear that laws were being broken and the risk of penalties severe, the timber cutting and railroad tie company was dissolved. Lee, Fall, Curry, and Hawkins returned to their regular routines. The father and son Llewellyns were, at the time, both federal employees. As a result of their involvement in the illegal activities, they lost their jobs.

Somehow, Pat Garrett learned of the timber harvesting operation on government property, the manufacture and sale of railroad ties, and the employment of illegal Chinese laborers. It has been assumed by some that Garrett wanted to be cut in on the scheme, as he was desperately in need of money. It is more likely, however, that Garrett would have been uncomfortable, even intimidated, being in a shady business with Lee and his associates, all of whom despised him. Garrett, as it turned out, was in a unique position to undertake revenge on his enemies by reporting their activities to the authorities. This notion, along with other ongoing difficulties, provided Oliver Lee additional reason to get rid of Pat Garrett.

CHAPTER 30

THE PLOT TO REMOVE PAT GARRETT

According to secret agent Fred Fornoff, the mastermind behind the plot to get Garrett out of the way was Oliver Lee, and Lee was provided with considerable input from his brother-in-law W. W. Cox, along with Print Rhode.

By this time Lee had developed a pattern for handling certain "business" difficulties. His principal business was his successful and growing ranching empire, but Lee dabbled in other enterprising ventures, the illegal smuggling of Chinese laborers and harvesting timber for railroad ties being two of them. When someone came forward in an attempt to interrupt or obstruct his moneymaking arrangements, or to represent the threat of an arrest, conviction, and jail term, Lee's modus operandi was to simply get rid of them.

As far as is known, the first official who undertook to charge Lee with wrongdoing was cattle detective Les Dow. Though significant time had passed and Lee escaped prosecution based on Dow's investigations, he knew the detective still possessed damaging evidence. Lee believed that the most efficient way to eliminate the problem was to remove the person involved. As a result, Les Dow was killed and rendered permanently out of the picture. Lee orchestrated Dow's murder, sending his trusted and loyal employee and nephew, Todd Bailey, to do the job.

James Leslie "Les" Dow was no lightweight. Before becoming a cattle inspector, he had a varied career that included a position as range detective and working as a New Mexico deputy sheriff in Chaves County. He also served as sheriff of Eddy County, New Mexico, and held an appointment as a US deputy marshal. Dow was no stranger to gunplay, having killed at least one man in a shootout.

According to at least three published accounts, Les Dow was killed by a man named Dave Kemp. Kemp had been a former sheriff of Eddy County, and new sheriff Dow suspected him of cattle rustling. Dow arrested Kemp, who was later released, and Kemp vowed revenge, a threat that was overheard by others. According to writers Metz, Jay Robert Nash, and Don Bullis, Kemp encountered Dow on February 16, 1897, and shot him in the face. The problem with each of these accounts is that they are the results of hearsay, and in at least one case the writer repeated previously published hearsay without establishing provenance. There were no witnesses to the shooting, and concentrated investigation into these versions has yielded that no such thing ever happened involving Kemp, the most likely suspect as a result of his earlier confrontation with Dow.

According to information in the possession of Todd Bailey's descendants, Oliver Lee, concerned that Dow still possessed evidence that could harm him, sent his nephew Todd Bailey to Carlsbad, Eddy County, New Mexico, to get rid of Dow. Bailey was accompanied by Killin' Jim Miller. The two men waited in hiding for Dow to come out of the post office. When he appeared, Bailey stepped up to him and shot him in the face with a revolver. Dow died the following day.

Next came Colonel Albert Jennings Fountain, the dogged prosecutor for the cattle association who was only days away from having Lee arrested and charged with cattle rustling and defacing brands. Lee knew he stood little chance in court, given the evidence possessed by Fountain, evidence initially gathered and supplied by Les Dow. The simplest way to handle this problem, in Lee's mind, was to get rid of Fountain.

The plan to kill Fountain was a slightly revised version of the one developed in 1894. Once again, the reliable and dependable crack shot Todd Bailey was enlisted. Fountain was dispatched, and it was unfortunate that eight-year-old Henry Fountain was along on the trip with his father, but Lee was determined to leave no witnesses. It was part of the cost of doing business.

And now, Pat Garrett, long a thorn in the side of Oliver Lee, was standing in the way of the Chinese smuggling venture and the railroad tie operation. Lee had had enough of Garrett and was determined to be rid of him once and for all. Now was the time.

In short, Pat Garrett's very existence affected the livelihood and safety of several prominent New Mexico citizens. It was decided that he had to be eliminated, and discussion ensued about the best way to accomplish this.

The plot to do away with Garrett was somewhat involved, and it included several participants. Investigator Fred Fornoff reported rumors he heard that rancher W. W. Cox was putting up an amount of money to have Pat Garrett killed. The contact man, according to Fornoff, was Mannen Clements, a part-time El Paso constable. Clements allegedly met with Cox in the El Paso law office of Albert B. Fall, where he was handed $1,500. Clements, as the rumors had it, was to use the money to hire Killin' Jim Miller to pull the trigger and to pay Carl Adamson to act as a witness. Cox would then talk to Wayne Brazel and convince him to take the blame for the killing, assuring the pliable cowhand that he would never be convicted.

Though rumors abound, historians, as a result of investigating and reporting by Fred Fornoff, generally agree that, prior to

Pat Garrett, 1898
RICHARD KOLB

the meeting with Cox and Clements, an earlier gathering was held at El Paso's St. Regis Hotel. In attendance were Oliver Lee, W. W. Cox, Albert B. Fall, Bill McNew, Jim Miller, Carl Adamson, Print Rhode, Mannen Clements, and Wayne Brazel. Most are convinced Cox called for the meeting. According to author Sonnichsen, Cox agreed to pay for the killing but stated that it needed to appear as an act of self-defense. Oliver Lee came up with a workable plan. Lee suggested that Wayne Brazel, a quiet, mild-mannered, and dependable ranch hand, lease Garrett's Bear Canyon Ranch from son Poe Garrett and place a herd of goats on it. Garrett hated goats, and when he learned of the transaction and confronted Brazel about it, as all knew he would, the ensuing disagreement would provide an excuse to kill him. It was agreed that any and all would be sympathetic to Brazel if he shot in "self-defense," and that it was unlikely that any jury would convict him. Because Brazel was not a killer and was unskilled and inexperienced in the use of firearms, someone else would have to perform the actual killing.

It was decided to get Garrett out of his home and away from his ranch to a remote location devoid of witnesses. To accomplish this, Carl Adamson, a partner in the smuggling operation, was elected to drive to his ranch, pick Garrett up in a buggy, and carry him to Las Cruces where Garrett believed he was to meet with Brazel. He was convinced that the meeting was called to break the lease with Brazel and facilitate the agreement to lease the Bear Canyon Ranch to Miller and Adamson. They presumed Garrett, badly needing money, would jump at the opportunity to do so.

On the way to Las Cruces, Garrett was to be ambushed. At a designated location, Adamson was to stop the buggy using the excuse that he had to urinate. Prior to halting the vehicle, Wayne Brazel, who would have positioned himself along the road, would ride up and engage Garrett in conversation as a distraction. Once the vehicle was stopped, Adamson was to climb down and Brazel was to back away, leaving Garrett isolated. From a vantage point, the shooter, using a rifle, would kill Garrett. Brazel would take the blame, confess to the killing, and plead self-defense. A witness, in the form of Adamson, the only other person present, was prepared to offer verification for Brazel's account.

The question was: Who was to be the shooter, the man to take down the once-famous lawman, Pat Garrett? Oliver Lee had the answer. He was close to a man who had the skill, a man who owed everything to, and would do anything for, his employer, a man who had killed before at Lee's request and would do it again this time. The shooter was to be Todd Bailey.

Some few writers insist that this meeting between Lee, Cox, and the others never took place and that the story was concocted out of whole cloth and repeated enough times to the point where history enthusiasts have accepted it as fact. While some are tempted to dismiss the entire affair as fiction, it must be pointed out that the source of the information was US deputy marshal Fred Fornoff, an experienced and well-respected investigator. In addition, a handful of interested individuals with backgrounds in criminal investigation suggest it is likely it did happen, for subsequent events provided verification.

CHAPTER 31

CARL ADAMSON

CARL ADAMSON REINED UP THE TEAM OF HORSES AND BROUGHT the buggy to a halt in front of the Garrett ranch house late on the afternoon of February 28, 1908. On hearing the arrival of company, Pat and Apolinaria stepped out onto the porch to greet him, and when Adamson climbed down from the vehicle they invited him inside. Apolinaria prepared coffee and served the two men as they visited. Days later, Mrs. Garrett confessed to harboring an uncomfortable suspicion about Adamson; she couldn't explain why but she thought him untrustworthy.

Coffee finished, Garrett invited Adamson for a stroll around a portion of his property, with the ex-lawman pointing out various features. During the stroll, Garrett mentioned that he had been wakened the previous night by his dogs barking at what appeared to be some kind of intrusion. Early in the morning, Garrett sent ranch hand Frank Adams out to investigate. In a nearby arroyo, Adams found the tracks of two men and horses. From the arroyo, there was a clear view of the Garrett ranch house.

Later while Adamson was tending to his horses, Mrs. Garrett pulled her husband aside and expressed her intuitions about their visitor. Garrett found her concerns amusing, and explained to her that Adamson was likely the key to their future financial independence. Earlier, after conferring with Adamson, Garrett had a message sent to Wayne Brazel indicating the necessity of meeting with him and Adamson in Las Cruces the next day.

The following morning, Apolinaria prepared a big breakfast for her husband and their guest. With the meal finished, Garrett and Adamson tossed their bags into the back of the vehicle. Garrett tied his saddled horse to the back of the buggy for the return trip, pulled on a pair of leather gloves, and placed a shotgun on the seat next to where he would sit. The shotgun was loaded with birdshot. This done, he and Adamson climbed onto the seat and set out for Las Cruces.

Garrett's young daughter Pauline stood on the front porch with her mother as the two men drove away. Apolinaria noted that Garrett had neglected to take his topcoat, and as the weather had the potential to get colder, she retrieved it, handed it to Pauline, and told her to run after the buggy and give it to him. Taking the garment, Pauline scrambled aboard her mare and raced down the road toward the departing vehicle. As the buggy slowed down on nearing a gate, Garrett heard Pauline's approach and told Adamson to stop. When the buggy halted, Garrett stepped to the ground, picked Pauline from her horse, and carried her over to the gate to unlatch it. He took the topcoat, kissed his daughter, and placed her back onto the mare. He told her he was going to bring her a present from Las Cruces. Pauline watched as her father and Adamson passed through the gate and saw her father relatch it. She turned and rode back to the house. It was the last time any of Garrett's family would see him alive.

CHAPTER 32
THE FINAL JOURNEY

THE BUGGY CARRYING PAT GARRETT AND CARL ADAMSON PRO-
ceeded at a steady pace along the dirt road to Las Cruces. The
route followed by Adamson passed through the community of
Gold Camp on the east side of the San Andres Mountains and
through the tiny village of Organ. Organ was another mining
camp located fourteen-and-a-half miles northeast of Las Cruces
and held a population of around fifteen hundred. A short distance
out of town, Adamson pulled up at Russell Walter's livery stable.
Garrett stepped out of the buggy and walked over to visit with
Willis Walter, the son of the proprietor. Adamson guided the
horses over to a water trough. According to an interview granted
by Walter in 1968, Garrett asked him if he had seen Wayne Brazel. This question seems odd since Garrett and Adamson were on
their way to Las Cruces to meet with Brazel.

Willis told Garrett that Brazel had been there but had ridden
away only minutes before the arrival of the buggy. Willis pointed
down the road at a column of dust that had apparently been
stirred up by Brazel's horse on the dry caliche road. As Garrett
and Willis Walter visited, Adamson pulled the horses back from
the trough and indicated to Garrett that he was ready to depart. A
moment later they were back on the road to Las Cruces.

South of Organ, the two men came to a fork in the road, the two routes extending more or less parallel for two miles before reconnecting. One of the roads was called the Mail-Scott Road and the other the Freighters' Road. The Freighters' Road was preferred by those who drove the heavy ore wagons. It was shorter but quite rough. Most travelers preferred the smoother Mail-Scott Road. As Adamson neared the junction, Garrett spotted Brazel on horseback several hundred yards down the Mail-Scott Road. He was in conversation with another man on horseback, one that Garrett, according to writers, could not identify. After a moment, the stranger turned his horse and galloped away down the road. Adamson steered the buggy onto the Mail-Scott Road

Historians and writers have suggested that the unidentified man was Print Rhode, one of Garrett's enemies and a man who had sworn to kill the ex-lawman. This notion was advanced in some of the earliest writings on the case and then repeated often throughout the ensuing years. While most who follow and/or wrote about Garrett's life and times have accepted this identification without question, it is at best a poor guess. If Garrett and Adamson were able to identify Wayne Brazel at that distance, then Rhode, who was well known to both men, would have been easily recognized. Accumulating evidence does not support the notion that the stranger was Print Rhode, but rather Todd Bailey, Oliver Lee's loyal nephew and ranch hand.

Todd Bailey spurred his horse down the Mail-Scott Road to a prearranged destination—a low ridge just to the south that paralleled the route. He guided his mount up the eastern spur of the ridge and on to the top. From a position near the western end of the ridge Bailey, sitting astride his horse, could observe the road from Organ and pick out travelers. A few moments later, he spotted the buggy transporting Garrett and Adamson.

Adamson and Garrett soon caught up with Brazel. Garrett despised Brazel, and the two men did little more than acknowledge each other's presence with a curt nod. For some distance, Brazel rode alongside the buggy; no words were exchanged between him and Garrett. According to subsequent reports in the *El Paso Herald* and the *Rio Grande Republican*, Brazel sometimes rode ahead of the buggy and sometimes behind it, and when the road was wide enough, he rode alongside it. Presently, Adamson asked Brazel if his goats were kidding.

As the buggy approached the low ridge, Bailey guided his horse down the south slope and out of sight from the road. At the bottom, he tied the animal to a low-growing mesquite tree. From a leather scabbard, he withdrew a .30 to .40 Krag, a lightweight lever-action carbine made by Winchester. The weapon, sporting a twenty-two-inch barrel and employed by the US Army since 1892, was loaded and ready for shooting with a .30 to .40 smokeless powder cartridge, one popular with hunters.

Rounding the western spur of the ridge on foot, Bailey made his way across the flat, a sand-gravel ground dotted with creosote bush and prickly pear. He crossed the area and proceeded another 130 feet to Alameda Arroyo. There, he walked toward a previously selected location in the shallow drainage, one that afforded a perfect field of fire. Brush and junipers lined the bank and grew thick in places between it and the road, but at the point where Bailey now stood there were no obstacles between him and the place where Adamson was to stop the buggy. While he waited, Bailey lit a hand-rolled cigarette and sat down on the bank of the arroyo.

It has been advanced by some that Killin' Jim Miller was also present in a separate but nearby location. Miller, it has been suggested, was along to serve as a backup shooter in the event something went wrong. While provocative, there exists no evidence that such was the case.

Finally growing annoyed and frustrated with Brazel's presence, Garrett spoke up and asked him why he originally stated he had twelve hundred goats on the leased property and later changed the number to eighteen hundred. Brazel replied that he had miscounted.

The difference between twelve hundred and eighteen hundred goats should strike any competent researcher as dramatic to the point of being unbelievable, but this disparity has never been addressed by historians and writers during the more than a century since Pat Garrett was killed. The fact that the goatherd was claimed to be 50 percent larger than previously believed should not be disregarded. The true number of goats originally placed on the Bear Canyon range would surely have been known to Brazel, Rhode, and Miller. Even allowing time for kidding, it remains unlikely that the herd would have grown to such a size in the amount of time that the goats had been in the canyon. This leads the investigator to ask the questions: Were these numbers cooked up to delay or obviate Garrett's potential opportunity to place Adamson's cattle on the range? Was Garrett being set up the entire time? If Garrett and Adamson had arranged to meet with Brazel and discuss the Bear Canyon lease in Las Cruces, then what was the ranch hand doing riding alongside the two men on the Mail-Scott Road?

Following the brief exchange between Garrett and Brazel, Adamson entered the conversation with the comment that he and Miller would not pay for eighteen hundred goats and that the deal might be cancelled. Adamson further stated that he did not want any of the goats, which he had only wanted to purchase to secure the lease. Brazel responded by stating that he would sell all eighteen hundred goats or none.

Seated on the bank of the arroyo, Bailey heard the jingle of traces and the clop of horse hooves on the road. From his position, he spotted the buggy a short distance away. Brazel was on horseback and maintaining a position to the right rear of the vehicle. Bailey could hear Garrett and Brazel arguing. Bailey tossed his cigarette to the ground, picked up the rifle, and readied himself. His target, the once-famous Pat Garrett, was almost in range.

CHAPTER 33
THE ASSASSINATION

As Adamson steered the buggy along a portion of the road that passed between the low ridge on the left and Alameda Arroyo on the right, he slowed, and then pulled to a halt, claiming he needed to urinate. He handed the lines to Garrett, stepped down from the buggy, and walked to a position in front of the horses. The fact that Adamson moved to the front of the horses rather than urinate by the side of the buggy where he stepped down represents an intriguing tell: It seems reasonable to assume that Adamson stationed himself such that he could grab the bridles of the animals should they be alarmed by a gunshot and try to bolt.

Garrett and Brazel were by this time shouting at one another. Garrett was no doubt concerned that the opportunity to lease the Bear Canyon ranch to Adamson and Miller for significant money was slipping away.

Brazel told Garrett that he was going to retain the lease. According to subsequent testimony by Adamson, Garrett responded by stating that he was going to get Brazel off his land one way or another.

At this Garrett, according to Adamson, set down the reins, picked up the shotgun he had brought with him, and stepped out of the buggy on the right side. Brazel remained on his horse on the opposite side of the buggy, backing it a few steps such that it was positioned behind the vehicle. Stepping a few paces to the side of the vehicle with the shotgun in his right hand, Garrett removed the glove from his left hand and unbuttoned his pants in order to urinate. Within another three seconds, he would be dead.

As Pat Garrett began to urinate, he was facing Brazel, his back toward the arroyo where Todd Bailey waited. Bailey raised the Krag, aimed, and fired. The bullet slammed into the back of Garrett's head not far from the left ear, tore through his brain, and exited at the right eyebrow. The tall man spun around, his arms flailing, and dropped to the ground. Bailey stated later that when Garrett hit the ground, the sound was "like you had dropped a sack of potatoes." Garrett was likely dead at this point.

When Garrett landed, his head was toward the buggy, his feet toward the arroyo. Calmly, Bailey ejected the shell, inserted another, took aim at the prone Garrett, and fired a second shot. The bullet entered Garrett's lower abdomen, proceeded at a low angle ripping through the torso, and came to lodge near the left shoulder and at the top of the rib cage.

Pat Garrett, a man who lived a life of adventure, a lawman and man hunter, a man who had enjoyed a level of fame and years of shame, was gone. For many, his death put an end to a number of concerns: Those to whom he owed money, and there were many, no longer had to wonder when they would be repaid; those whom he pursued such as Oliver Lee, Jim Gilliland, Bill McNew, and Albert Fall could rest a little easier; those who despised Garrett for any number of reasons would no longer be bothered by his existence.

For those who wondered who might have killed the once famous lawman, the mysteries surrounding his assassination were only beginning.

PART IV
AFTERMATH

CHAPTER 34
CONFESSION

LEAVING THE CORPSE OF PAT GARRETT LYING WHERE HE FELL, Wayne Brazel and Carl Adamson continued on to Las Cruces. On arriving in the town, Brazel stepped into the sheriff's office and approached Deputy Felipe Lucero. With little preamble, Brazel confessed to shooting and killing Pat Garrett and told the deputy to lock him up. Brazel unbuckled his holster rig containing a .45-caliber Colt revolver and handed it over to Lucero. He informed the deputy that Adamson was present at the killing and that he would testify that it was done in self-defense, that Garrett was about to shoot him with his shotgun. Lucero placed Brazel in a cell.

Following the arrest of Wayne Brazel, Lucero assembled a coroner's jury, and once this was accomplished, all rode out to the site of the killing. Following an examination by Dr. W. C. Field, Garrett's body was loaded into a wagon and transported to Las Cruces. There, Field performed an autopsy.

Following the coroner's jury to the assassination site was former New Mexico militiaman W. H. H. Llewellyn. At 2:22 p.m. on March 4, Llewellyn sent a telegram to New Mexico governor George Curry stating that, "Wayne Brazel killed Pat Garrett about noon five miles from Las Cruces on Organ Road." The second line of the telegram added one of the first layers of mystery to the event. Llewellyn wrote that "Garrett and Miller were in buggy, Brazel on horseback. Brazel in jail here."

Llewellyn's mention of Miller, presumably "Killin' Jim" Miller, is puzzling. Here are the facts: Carl Adamson drove Garrett from his ranch house that morning, Adamson was with Garrett when the two men stopped at Walter's livery outside of the town of Organ, and Adamson showed up at the sheriff's office in Las Cruces with Brazel following the killing. So where did Llewellyn come up with the notion that Miller was in the buggy with Garrett?

There is another problem with Llewellyn's telegram. It has been established that he was in Las Cruces at the time of the killing. There is no way he could have visited the assassination site and returned to Las Cruces to send a telegram at 2:22 p.m. This appears to be the beginning of an ever-widening web of entanglements associated with the killing of Pat Garrett.

Did Llewellyn simply make a mistake and state Miller's name instead of Adamson's? It would be difficult to confuse the two men. Did Llewellyn hear something that caused him to mention Miller's name? If so, from whom? Was Llewellyn privy to information that was missed by historians and writers? The truth behind these questions may never be known.

On March 3, Brazel was escorted into the courtroom of Justice of the Peace Manuel Lopez. When asked how he wished to plead to the charge of murder, Brazel appeared confused and was described as having a blank stare on his face. He asked that the question be repeated, and when it was, he pled not guilty, "then resumed his vacant staring."

That same afternoon, a hearing for Brazel was arranged. Mark Thompson was the prosecuting attorney for Doña Ana County and was assisted by New Mexico attorney general James M. Hervey and Governor George Curry. New Mexico mounted policeman Fred Fornoff, on learning of Garrett's assassination, arrived from Santa Fe to attend the funeral and was invited to take part in the proceedings. Leading the defense of Brazel was Albert B. Fall, the personal attorney of rancher W. W. Cox, Brazel's employer, as well as of Oliver Lee. Assisting Fall were Herbert B. Holt, William A. Sutherland, and Edward C. Wade. The presence of four attorneys for the defense was an unusual event. When Cox arrived, he remained at Brazel's side throughout the entire proceedings. Oddly, Holt had been Garrett's attorney.

When Adamson was called to testify, he stated that he stopped the buggy to urinate. Before climbing down from the vehicle, he handed the reins to Garrett. While he was standing near the horses, Adamson said he heard Garrett and Brazel arguing, heard Garrett say, "Well, damn you. If I don't get you off one way, I will another." During the argument, according to Adamson, Garrett was in the buggy and Brazel was on horseback near the left side. Adamson claimed his back was turned to the pair.

When an attorney asked Adamson if he had seen Garrett standing upright, he replied, "I think when I seen Garrett, the first shot had been fired and he was staggering," and that he fell "about two feet from the side of the buggy." Brazel was on horseback where he had been, according to Adamson, but he was now holding a revolver.

The attorney asked who fired the second shot. Adamson only replied, "One of my horses started to run and I grabbled the lines and wrapped them as quickly as I could around the hub of the wheel and went back to where Mr. Garrett lay."

When Dr. Field was called to the stand, he stated that Garrett had no glove on his left hand and that his trousers were unbuttoned and stained with urine. It was clear to Field that Garrett was urinating at the time he was shot in the head. Field opined that the evidence pointed to murder in "cold blood and in the first degree."

Attorney General Hervey set Brazel's bond at $10,000. W. W. Cox left the building and circulated through town raising money from businessmen, cattlemen, and private citizens. He had no difficulty coming up with enough.

On April 13, the grand jury indicted Wayne Brazel for murder. His trial was scheduled for April 19, 1909, one year after the death of Pat Garrett.

CHAPTER 35

THE TRIAL OF WAYNE BRAZEL

IN COURT, WAYNE BRAZEL TESTIFIED THAT GARRETT HAD threatened him with his shotgun and that he had no choice but to shoot first. In contradiction to Field's testimony that Garrett had been shot in the back of the head, Brazel insisted that he was facing him at the time.

Author Leon Metz wrote that the "case was prosecuted with appalling indifference and incompetence." Adamson, who was the only witness of record at the time of the shooting, did not even appear in court to testify; he was serving a term in jail for smuggling Chinese laborers into the country. It was learned that, following the assassination, telegrams were sent back and forth between Brazel, Adamson, W. W. Cox, Print Rhode, and Jim Miller, all Garrett haters. The communications were subpoenaed, but were never produced.

Prosecuting Attorney Thompson argued that if Garrett had intended to shoot Brazel, that he would have loaded his shotgun with buckshot and not the birdshot that it carried. He also suggested that Garrett would likely have fired at Brazel from the buggy seat instead of descending to the ground.

The case was turned over to the jurors at 5:30 p.m. They returned in an astonishing fifteen minutes with a verdict of "not guilty." That evening, a grand party was held for Brazel at the W. W. Cox ranch.

Formally, Wayne Brazel was found innocent of the killing of Pat Garrett as a result of self-defense. Within hours of learning of Garrett's murder, whisperings and rumors circulated throughout southeastern New Mexico that Brazel could not have been the shooter. Those who knew the mild-mannered cowhand claimed he was not capable of such a thing, that he possessed neither the mentality nor the wherewithal for killing. It was pointed out that Brazel rarely carried a revolver, and when he did he was a notoriously poor shot. Attention soon turned to others, all suspects in the killing. All of them, according to the accusers, were capable of murder, and all had something to gain with the death of Pat Garrett.

CHAPTER 36
THE SUSPECTS

For years, the killing of Pat Garrett swirled in controversy. The once famous lawman whose life was linked to controversial events such as his alleged killing of Billy the Kid and the disappearance of Albert Jennings Fountain, along with his numerous failed get-rich-quick-schemes, became mired in difficulties and contention once again, this time in death.

In the numerous published accounts of the assassination of Pat Garrett, the vast majority of them credit the deed to Brazel. As a result of the court's finding that Wayne Brazel was not guilty in the death of Pat Garrett by reason of self-defense, writers have incorporated that decision into their treatments of the event, in spite of charges of "incompetence" and the strong suspicion that lawmakers as well as jurors may have been influenced to some degree or another by moneyed and influential members of the anti-Garrett faction, including Albert B. Fall, W. W. Cox, Oliver Lee, and others. Those skeptical of the jury trial and the testimony find few reasons to convince them that Brazel pulled the trigger, and other names were advanced as the real or potential killers. They included: Carl Adamson, W. W. Cox, Print Rhode, and Jim Miller. Oddly, Todd Bailey was not among those who were suspected of being involved, though it seems he was a clear and obvious choice.

Todd Bailey's role in the assassination of Pat Garrett was never mentioned in print until 2013; he was there all the time, but the so-called experts passed him over.

An examination of those identified as suspects in the killing of Pat Garrett is warranted.

CARL ADAMSON

For years, members of the Garrett family were convinced that Carl Adamson was the killer. Adamson generated an uncomfortable response from Apilonaria Garrett when he arrived at the ranch to transport the victim to Las Cruces to meet with Brazel. Further, the family claimed, he was the only other person at the scene of the crime.

Although it is clear that Adamson was involved in the plot to assassinate Garrett, he is probably the easiest of the named suspects to dismiss as the assassin. Despite the claims of the Garrett family members, there exists not a single shred of evidence that Adamson was the shooter. Adamson was a close acquaintance of W. W. Cox and Oliver Lee, and it has been established that he was involved with those men and others in smuggling Chinese laborers across the United States–Mexico border. Once the immigrants were across, the smugglers needed a place to house them before shipping them to Colorado where they had been contracted to work in the mines. Garrett's Bear Canyon property was deemed the ideal location to house the illegals, thus Adamson had a vested interest in removing Garrett from the determinations. The truth is, however, that Adamson and Garrett got along well and there had never been any animosity between the two men.

Further, while Adamson was surely attracted to the possibility that a significant amount of money might be forthcoming from the plot to smuggle Chinese laborers, the truth is he had no background whatsoever relative to killing anyone. Greed, and the potential for wealth, however, has often been documented as a motive for murder. Still, there exists no logical reason why Adamson could be considered the murderer of Pat Garrett.

W. W. COX

A man named W. T. Moyers practiced law in New Mexico during the time of Pat Garrett's assassination. Several years later he moved to Colorado where he claimed he conducted research into the killing. As a result of his efforts, Moyers became convinced that W. W. Cox had shot and killed Garrett. Moyers passed his revelations on to Fred M. Mazzulla, a collector of Old West photography, and suggested that he write up the story and sell it for $5,000, which they would split. Nothing ever came of the project, and if Moyers possessed incriminating evidence regarding Cox's role in the death of Garrett, it never surfaced.

Cox's alleged motives for killing Garrett, or having him killed, relate to the notions that (1) he wanted Garrett's land and water, (2) he hated Garrett for the disturbance he created at his ranch when he killed Norman Newman, (3) he was concerned that Garrett was getting close to solving the Fountain disappearance, which would have greatly affected his good friend and in-law, Oliver Lee, and (4) Garrett had the potential to disrupt the potentially lucrative smuggling of Chinese laborers. These notions invite examination.

If Cox had wanted to obtain possession of Garrett's land, he could have done so legally and with a minimum of difficulty for he held notes on the property. Furthermore, Garrett's ranch had fallen into disrepair and had been described as "poverty stricken." It is doubtful that Cox would have longed for such a property when he already had his hands full with his own extensive holdings. Near the end of 1908, Cox wound up taking possession of Garrett's ranch based on the notes. When it came time for Mrs.

Garrett and the family to be moved from the ranch, Cox assisted her and provided her with a sum of money.

Related to Garrett's land, the alleged scheme of Cox being behind the placing of goats on the Bear Canyon property to provoke him into what was intended to be a life-ending dispute is fraught with contradictions. If such were Cox's plan, he would have the means to fund the operation, which he didn't do. The truth is that Wayne Brazel borrowed money from Cox and signed a promissory note to repay it in a year. With Brazel's difficulties related to the trial, as well as trying to tend to his goat herd, he was unable to repay the loan. A year after lending Brazel the money, Cox lent him another $300 for attorney fees. The terms stated that the loan had to be repaid within ninety days at 10 percent interest. After four years of holding Brazel's debts and not receiving any money, Cox filed suit to collect, but was unsuccessful. Brazel was unable to pay his debts and Cox eventually dropped all of his efforts to get his money.

Regarding the fight with and the killing of Norman Newman, Cox never manifested any degree of anger toward Garrett relative to the incident, not like Print Rhode. During the months following the incident, Cox and Garrett encountered one another from time to time and the subject was never brought up.

It is highly likely that Cox was aware of the role of Oliver Lee in the disappearance and death of Albert Jennings Fountain. If Cox was concerned that Garrett was still interested in pursuing an investigation into the matter, it apparently did not disturb him. Cox was aware of Garrett's shoddy investigation of the case, and nothing about the ex-lawman indicated that he would have any success in reopening it.

Cox knew that Garrett did indeed have the potential to disrupt the scheme to smuggle Chinese laborers. Given the circumstances, the only solution, one agreed upon by all involved, was to get rid of Garrett. Cox was a long time removed geographically and chronologically from the violence he experienced in Texas as a young man; as a well known and respected rancher in this region of southern New Mexico, pulling the trigger on Garrett was not his style, nor could it be considered an efficient move since he had at his disposal more efficient and experienced killers in Todd Bailey and Jim Miller.

PRINT RHODE

Other than the fact that Print Rhode had sworn to kill Garrett in front of witnesses, no evidence of any substance links him with the assassination. Rhode despised Garrett for a long time, and his distaste for the lawman went back ten years to the disturbance at the Cox ranch when Norman Newman was killed.

The Newman-related event hardly seems a reason to kill someone, even for an oft-described hothead like Rhode. While it is true that Rhode was involved in the goat ranching operation, the complications of that scheme have already been discussed. Furthermore, Rhode had ample opportunity to kill Garrett in the ten years that had elapsed since the Newman incident, but he made no such move. No aspect of Print Rhode as a suspect in the killing of Pat Garrett carries with it any logic or credibility whatsoever.

KILLIN' JIM MILLER

A number of historians and outlaw/lawman enthusiasts are eager to point to Killin' Jim Miller as Garrett's assassin, and over the years he has gradually risen to the top of the list of suspects in the minds of several researchers. Miller had been a notorious, colorful, and attention-generating character, as well as a well-known and oft-hired assassin. As a suspect, Miller requires close examination.

In the days leading up to Garrett's assassination, Miller posed as a rancher and cattleman, but he was neither. The Miller-as-killer supporters employ this connection, stating that it was a ruse he used to get close to Garrett. If Miller had been the killer, why would he have involved a complicated tactic such as this when all he needed to do was hide behind a bush and shoot a man while he was urinating? The assumption is unreasonable.

According to author Metz, the "attempt to place Miller at the death site is based on the discovery of a Winchester cartridge case along with horse tracks and droppings in the murder area." It is difficult to impossible to discern any tangible links to these observations and Miller. For one thing, Miller's long-preferred killing weapon was a shotgun, not a rifle. Since the road taken by Adamson, Brazel, and Garrett was well traveled, it should come as no surprise that someone might encounter horse tracks and droppings. Further, the .45-caliber shell casing found by Doña Ana County medical examiner Field could have come from anybody and could have been fired as a result of a hunting venture long before Garrett, Adamson, and Brazel arrived at the location.

There exists a reported incident that many Miller-as-assassin devotees refer to in an attempt to support their position that he was the killer of Pat Garrett. A man named Joe Beasley told an investigator that while he was working at his job on a ranch, Killin' Jim Miller passed through on the morning of the assassination and stated that he intended to kill Pat Garrett and asked to borrow a horse. On returning the horse the next day, Miller allegedly told Beasley that he had killed Garrett.

The problem with this account is that Joe Beasley possessed no credibility whatsoever. Beasley was described as a "character," and had been convicted of a number of crimes over the years. According to author Metz, Beasley "made a specialty of perjuring himself in court for wanted criminals." Further, it is doubtful that

Miller would have announced to Beasley, of all people, any intention of killing someone.

Another thing enthusiasts like to quote when presenting and promoting Miller as Garrett's assassin is his alleged confession of the deed just before he was hanged in Ada, Oklahoma, on April 19, 1909. Such a thing never happened. Walter Gayne, who was Miller's jailer when the outlaw was dragged from his cell and strung up from a barn rafter, stated that Miller mentioned neither Garrett nor his role in much of anything before he died. According to author C. L. Sonnichsen, Gayne said, "I ought to know because I hung him."

WAYNE BRAZEL

The final suspect that bears examination is Wayne Brazel, the man who confessed to the crime of killing Pat Garrett and who was found not guilty in a court of law. In spite of the inconsistencies related to Brazel's role in Garrett's death, author Metz writes, "A thorough examination of the many theories, all the evidence now obtainable, leads one to the inescapable conclusion that [Brazel] was, indeed, the killer of Pat Garrett." To this day, many are convinced that Brazel was the killer based in large part on Metz's pronouncement. Metz could not have been more mistaken; Wayne Brazel did not kill Pat Garrett.

By the time Metz's book on Pat Garrett was published in 1974, "a thorough examination of the many" theories had not been conducted by him or anyone else. A number of cursory analyses were processed, some by Metz himself, but none that contained any substance whatsoever. Metz was a competent writer, but his research was often disorganized and incomplete. To Metz, research amounted to little more than looking up previously published material and repeating it. Nowhere in his analyses and interpretations can one find an example of where he conducted an in-depth investigation.

Metz was further handicapped by two things: He only had at his fingertips, as he stated, "the evidence now obtainable." Since his book was published, additional evidence has come to light. It is also clear that Pat Garrett was elevated to the status of hero by Metz, one who sought glorification and worked hard to keep from being exposed for what he was, a man who craved admiration for his many alleged accomplishments. Metz emphasized this stand in print and in a number of presentations and conversations throughout the years.

There are several compelling reasons why Wayne Brazel should be dismissed as the killer of Garrett in addition to the evidence that ties Todd Bailey to the assassination. For one, Brazel testified in court that he shot Garrett in the head while facing him. Dr. W. C. Field, the head of the coroner's jury and a man experienced in such things, observed that Garrett had been shot in the back of the head just below the hat line, the bullet traveling on a straight plane and exiting at the right eyebrow. Field noted that graying brown hair at the back of Garrett's head had been carried into the skull and mixed with the destroyed brain matter. Brazel lied.

The term "hat line" is arbitrary, and in this case meaningless. No one knows how Pat Garrett was wearing his hat at the time he was shot. It could have been tipped up in front, or pulled down, or even cocked to the side.

Garrett had climbed down off the right side of the buggy. He took at least a couple of steps, removed the glove from his left hand, and turned toward Brazel who was still on horseback on the opposite side of the vehicle. As the argument between Garrett and Brazel continued, the ex-lawman unbuttoned his trousers and was facing his adversary as he was urinating. Behind Garrett was a shallow arroyo. The shot struck Garrett from behind. The first shot, the one that killed Garrett, was not fired by Wayne Brazel, but by the shooter in the arroyo—Todd Bailey.

After the bullet tore through his skull, the force of the impact caused Garrett to wheel around and fall to the ground onto his back, his feet toward the arroyo. A second bullet entered Garrett's lower abdomen and plowed at a shallow angle through his upper body, ending its journey near the left shoulder. Brazel did not fire this shot. For him to have accomplished this, he would have had to dismount, walk around the buggy, kneel down near Garrett's feet and, holding his revolver at a nearly horizontal angle, shoot the already dead man in the stomach. Brazel did no such thing, if his intention was to apply a coup de grâce, it would have been far easier and logical to shoot Garrett in the head or the heart from a standing position.

Brazel testified that Garrett was about to shoot him with his shotgun when he, Brazel, drew his revolver and shot first. Garrett's shotgun was loaded with birdshot, hardly the kind of ammunition one would load into a shotgun if his intention was to kill someone. In addition, during the act of urinating, Garrett was hardly in a position to shoot anyone with a shotgun. Further, when the party consisting of Lucero, Field, and others arrived from Las Cruces, it was noted that the shotgun was *still encased in its scabbard and was unloaded.* Given these facts, it is not likely that Brazel would have felt sufficiently threatened by Garrett that he would shoot him and plead self-defense.

The only "inescapable conclusion," as Metz puts it, would be that Brazel did not kill Pat Garrett. This sequence does not even demand a "thorough investigation," as Metz suggested he had conducted. Even a cursory examination of the facts related to the event reveals that Brazel could not have been the killer. None of the so-called evidence leading toward Brazel as the assassin of Pat Garrett carries any logic whatsoever. Indeed, the evidence is strongly *against* Brazel as the shooter.

The obvious question to be asked is: Why, then, did Brazel admit to killing Pat Garrett when the evidence demonstrates that he did not? Given the circumstances related to the shooting, taken in context with subsequent events, it becomes clear that Brazel, who did not pull the trigger, was nevertheless part of a plot to do away with Garrett. Evidence strongly suggests that the plot involved W. W. Cox, Oliver Lee, Print Rhode, Jim Miller, Carl Adamson, and Todd Bailey. Brazel, extraordinarily loyal to rancher Cox, had agreed to participate and take the fall, for all involved knew that he, more than anyone else, would stand the best chance of being found innocent of the charge of murder and would never serve a day in prison.

CHAPTER 37

THE PLOT TO KILL PAT GARRETT REVISITED

When Pat Garrett was assassinated, Fred Fornoff was serving as a captain in the New Mexico Mounted Police. Born in Baltimore, Maryland, in 1859, Fornoff traveled west as a young man and found work as a miner, a brick maker, and day laborer. He served in the Spanish-American War as one of Theodore Roosevelt's Rough Riders. On returning stateside, Fornoff became the city marshal of Albuquerque. Following that he held positions as a deputy US marshal, a Secret Service agent, and a special investigator for the Justice Department. As a lawman, Fornoff earned a reputation as a solid investigator and man hunter.

On March 1, 1908, Fornoff traveled to Las Cruces for the funeral of Pat Garrett. Accompanying him was New Mexico governor George Curry and Attorney General James M. Hervey. Curry had been invited to be one of the pallbearers.

While in the area, Fornoff visited the murder site. Several weeks later, Governor Curry instructed Fornoff to conduct an investigation into the assassination, as well as the circumstances leading up to it. Later, Fornoff's notes on the case, including his findings, were given to Mounted Police office clerk Page B. Otero for typing. The final draft was titled "The Fornoff Report." In

August 1908, the report was forwarded to Governor Curry, who in turn passed it on to Attorney General Hervey for his review and comments.

On learning of the existence of the report, the *El Paso Herald* requested a copy of it. Hervey claimed that the report was to be used in the upcoming trial of Wayne Brazel, must remain confidential until that time, and refused the newspaper. Subsequent investigation revealed that the report was never entered into the trial proceedings and Fornoff was never asked to testify about any part of his investigation.

Several weeks after Brazel's trial, Attorney General Hervey left public service and returned to private practice. While moving out of his office, he took all of his personal papers, along with a number of others marked "confidential." One of these was the Fornoff Report. When Hervey passed away in 1953, Charles Brice, his law partner, assumed possession of his papers. When Brice died in 1963, all of the materials were passed on to his family. Since none of the papers meant anything to them, they carried them to the Roswell city dump and burned them. It is believed that the only extant copy of the Fornoff Report was among them.

During the 1960s, Fred Lambert, the last living member of the New Mexico Mounted Police, was living in Cimarron, New Mexico. Lambert told an interviewer that he had read Fornoff's field notes as well as the final draft of the report typed by Page Otero. The interviewer asked Lambert to reveal what was in the notes, but he answered, "Let it be. The families of these men are respectable now. Let the closets stay closed."

During a series of subsequent interviews, however, Lambert was agreeable to revealing portions of the report. Lambert also admitted that in 1912, he and Fred Fornoff discussed in detail the murder of Pat Garrett.

Lambert also explained that in the weeks before Wayne Brazel's trial, and continuing on through 1913, certain lawmakers invested a great deal of effort to abolish the New Mexico Mounted Police. The attempt failed, but the force was cut in half. Lambert asked Fornoff why the legislators wanted to eliminate the police. Fornoff replied, "They know I know about the Garrett plot and the big money interests behind the Fountain killings. As long as the police exist, they are in danger. [If there are] no police, [then] there is less danger of any new evidence seeing daylight." Fornoff then outlined for Lambert the plan and motive that likely resulted in the death of Pat Garrett. The original idea, according to Fornoff, was to ruin Garrett financially, take his property, and then force him to leave the area. The scheme, he suggested, generated a momentum that eventually led to his murder. Fornoff was partly correct.

During his years as a US deputy marshal and Secret Service agent, Fornoff developed a number of close relationships with high-level federal officials. These officials told Fornoff that they were developing a case against a group of men involved in smuggling illegal Chinese laborers out of Mexico through Texas, into the state of New Mexico, and on to the mines and farms in southern Colorado. Men involved in the plot, as it was related to Fornoff, included Oliver Lee, W. W. Cox, Carl Adamson, Print Rhode, Mannen Clements, and likely others including Jim Miller.

Much of the information pertaining to the smuggling operation came from the physician, Dr. W. C. Field, the man who led the coroner's jury in Garrett's murder investigation and performed the autopsy on the body. Field had treated one of the smuggled Chinese for some ailment while he was housed at the county jail in Las Cruces. The prisoner revealed the smuggling arrangements to Field and named the suspects. Field wrote a letter to US Marshal Creighton Foraker and included all of this information. Foraker passed the missive on to other federal agents. It was at this point that Fornoff undertook his investigation.

Fornoff learned that after the illegal Chinese crossed the Mexican border they needed a safe and remote location to hide out until such time as they could be transported to Colorado. Garrett's Bear Canyon ranch suited this purpose, but unfortunately for the smugglers, Wayne Brazel and Print Rhode were already occupying the site for their goat ranching operation. Because Garrett was convinced that Carl Adamson and Jim Miller wanted the location to hold cattle they claimed they were bringing up from Mexico, he was desperate to remove Brazel, Rhode, and their goats. The truth was that Adamson and Miller had no cattle; they wanted the location to hide the Chinese.

It was inevitable that Garrett would discover that Adamson and Miller had no cattle. The two men considered revealing their plans to Garrett and offering a piece of the action. Since Garrett was deeply in debt, they presumed he would jump at the chance to make some money. The biggest obstacle to the plan, however, was that when Garrett learned that his longtime enemies Oliver Lee and Print Rhode, as well as men to whom he owed money such as W. W. Cox, were involved in the plot, he would not only refuse to participate but would likely alert law enforcement authorities. These very men had to some degree or another tormented Garrett in the past, and it was feared the old lawman would seize the opportunity to take revenge. To the men involved in the smuggling operation, there appeared to be only one solution to their predicament: Pat Garrett had to be eliminated. Fornoff was on target with his analysis.

As a result of his investigation, Fornoff was convinced that the principal men behind the plot to get Garrett out of the way were Oliver Lee, Print Rhode, and W. W. Cox, all brothers-in-law. It was rumored that when Garrett earlier connected Lee and Cox to the killing of Albert Jennings Fountain and his son, Henry, Cox agreed to finance the killing of Garrett. People had to be paid off, it was assumed, and Wayne Brazel was one of them. Brazel was convinced by Cox to confess to the crime with the assurance that he would never go to prison. To assist in this part of the plot, Cox contacted his own personal attorney to represent Brazel at the trial. That lawyer was Albert B. Fall.

Oliver Lee provided the gunman for the assassination, a man who had long proven his loyalty and devotion to the rancher: his nephew and trusted ranch hand, Todd Bailey.

Had the Fornoff Report been released to be entered into the trial of Wayne Brazel, the published history of the assassination of Pat Garrett would likely have been quite different from what it is today. An important question to be asked is: Why was the Fornoff Report not released? Speculation abounds, with some suggesting that the money and influence wielded by W. W. Cox, with perhaps some pressure applied from Albert Fall and Oliver Lee, affected the decision. Others simply credit the inexpert and inept law enforcement and judicial officials who were ubiquitous in that time and place. Whatever the truth, it is unlikely we will ever know.

EPILOGUE: THE UNFOLDING YEARS

Following the death of Pat Garrett, and thus the elimination of a real and potential threat to several individuals with involvement in previous and ongoing criminal activities in south-central New Mexico, life continued to unfold there and elsewhere with considerably less drama than the citizens had heretofore been subjected to. Life for the participants in a number of the region's greatest mysteries, murders, and other events settled into a pattern of routine, with a few, such as Oliver Lee, branching out into politics, and others continuing with their ranching and business enterprises. Others simply vanished without a trace.

OLIVER LEE

Though many believed at the time, and subsequent evidence has revealed, that Oliver Milton Lee played a dominant role in the assassinations of Pat Garrett, Albert J. Fountain and his young son Henry, as well as several others who threatened to interfere with his livelihood, he spoke little about these events during the remainder of his life. When Pat Garrett was brought up in conversation, Lee always refused to revisit the subject.

Lee continued to operate his ranches while living in his Dog Canyon home. As a competent and intelligent rancher, he enjoyed numerous successes, and enjoyed a level of prominence among area cattlemen. Lee eventually became acquainted with a man named McNary, an influential El Paso, Texas, banker, who purchased his ranch. McNary talked Lee into remaining as manager of the large Circle Cross ranching operation, with headquarters established near Tiburon, New Mexico. At the time, it was the largest ranch in the state. Several months later, however, McNary's bank failed, this disaster followed by financial difficulties, and Lee found himself idled.

In 1919, Lee had agreed to accompany noted race car driver Johnny Hutchings on a cross-country competition from El Paso to Phoenix, Arizona. The race was highly publicized, as was Lee's presence. When Hutchings's car, with Lee in the passenger seat, reached a point thirty miles west of El Paso, Army major William F. Scanland, an observer standing alongside the route, stepped forward and fired a shot into the car. The bullet struck and mortally wounded Hutchings. Scanland was arrested, tried, convicted, and sent to prison. Rumors abounded implying that Oliver Lee had been the intended target. The relationship between Scanland and Lee, if one ever existed, was never investigated or verified.

Lee moved to Alamogordo, and soon afterward was named director of the Federal Land Bank. He ran for and was elected to several terms in the New Mexico state legislature from 1918 through 1930, thrice as a representative and thrice as a senator. In 1932, he ran for New Mexico state land commissioner on the Republican ticket and was soundly defeated.

In 1941, Lee suffered a stroke at the age of seventy-six. He died on December 15 of that year. Several descendants of Oliver Lee continue to live and ranch in New Mexico today.

JIM GILLILAND

Several years following the disappearance of Albert Jennings Fountain and his son, Henry, Jim Gilliland purchased a ranch sixty-five miles northwest of Alamogordo. It was rumored that on several occasions throughout the remainder of his life, Jim Gilliland admitted his role in the abduction of the Fountains and his killing of eight-year-old Henry. Initially, Gilliland bragged about his involvement, and claimed that everyone was better off without Fountain around. During his later years, however, it was said that when Gilliland talked about killing young Henry Fountain he cried openly and expressed regret. It was reported that Gilliland drank heavily in the hope that it would help him forget.

Another story that made the rounds claimed that Gilliland had arranged a meeting with a Las Cruces lawyer who wrote down his confession and notarized it. Further, members of the Gilliland family revealed that Jim had kept a diary that was filled with details of the Fountain killings, with special attention given to his role in cutting Henry Fountain's throat. The notarized confession, as well as the diary, is in the possession of Gilliland descendants who, at this writing, refuse to have it made public.

In 1916, Gilliland, who assisted in burying the bodies of Albert and Henry Fountain in a remote canyon in the San Andres Mountains, grew concerned that the gravesite would remain unmarked. Likely out of guilt, according to some, he traveled to the location and marked the location with a large rock.

As an elderly man and unable to keep up with the obligations and hard work associated with ranching sixty-three thousand acres, he sold his property and operation in 1937 to a man named Butler Oral Burris, who went by the nickname "Snook." Burris had known Oliver Lee and rancher W. W. Cox, and eventually became friends with Gilliland. Following the sale of his ranch, Gilliland remained on site for two months to assist Burris in gathering the cattle. During that time, the two men enjoyed long conversations, and Burris learned a lot about Gilliland's past and his role in the Fountain murders. Gilliland eventually moved to Hot Springs, New Mexico. (Today, Hot Springs is known as Truth or Consequences.) He passed away there within a year.

During a 1969 interview with author Leon Metz, Oral Burris stated that Gilliland, at around seventy-five years of age, was in relatively good health, was very alert, and remained active, though he walked with a stoop. He described Gilliland as six-feet-four-inches tall and weighing about 250 pounds.

At one point during their brief relationship, Gilliland handed Burris a "Masonic pin, very rare . . . with an Odd Fellows link on the bottom of it." Gilliland told Burris he took the pin off the body of Colonel Albert Jennings Fountain. He asked Burris to return it to Albert Fountain Jr. on the event of his death. Gilliland passed away on August 8, 1948. Burris placed the pin in a safe deposit box for a time, and eventually saw that it was handed over to Fountain family members. According to Burris, "The family traced it for positive proof that it was the pin of [Colonel] Fountain," and identified it as having belonged to him.

Burris stated that Gilliland admitted killing young Henry Fountain; that he "just got him by the hair of the head and cut his little old throat." According to Burris, Gilliland said, "I can still see that little fellow, but dead men tell no tales."

WILLIAM MCNEW

A longtime friend and business and ranching partner of Oliver Lee, Bill McNew was described as having "ice-blue eyes" and was "the meanest, most murderous, and least forgiving of the trio consisting of him, Lee, and Gilliland."

Following the Fountain incident, McNew remained in ranching, eventually moving to San Marcial in Socorro County, New Mexico. It was said that McNew brought bad luck to the small community. During his time there, the town was destroyed on two occasions, once as a result of flooding from the nearby Rio Grande and again as a result of fire. McNew then moved to Ancho, a tiny community in Lincoln County.

Author Leon Metz encountered an odd story concerning McNew. During the late spring of 1937, McNew suffered a stroke and, as no heartbeat could be detected, was declared to be dead. He was laid on a mortician's table to be prepared for burial when he suddenly regained consciousness. Several days later when he was able to talk, he told family members that while he was unconscious he had strange dreams. He said he saw himself in hell and was "standing up to his knees in molten lava."

A few weeks later on June 30, McNew had another stroke from which he died. Just prior to passing away, however, it was reported that his lower legs had manifested severe blisters and the skin peeled way as though it had been burned.

BILL CARR

Bill Carr, along with William McNew, was investigated relative to the disappearance of the Fountains and Henry. Both men were eventually released from custody at a formal hearing. Following this, Carr was said to have had a religious conversion at a tent revival and allegedly became overtly pious. Shortly thereafter, Carr would advance to the pulpit of many a subsequent revival or church service and deliver testimonials that reportedly revealed his role in the kidnapping and killing of the Fountains. Hearing of this, Oliver Lee, William McNew, Jim Gilliland, and others began to grow concerned and debated whether or not something needed to be done about their former partner. As it turned out, Carr was regarded by most who heard him testify as half-mad and few paid any attention to his incoherent ramblings.

ALBERT BACON FALL

In 1912, Albert Bacon Fall, longtime lawyer for Oliver Lee and W. W. Cox, was elected to the US Senate on the Republican ticket, and reelected in 1918. As a senator, Fall served as chairman of the Committee on Expenditures in the Department of Commerce and Labor. In March 1921, he was appointed secretary of the interior by President Warren G. Harding. Fall's department was given the responsibility for the Naval Reserves land at Elk Hills and Buena Vista, California, and at Teapot Dome, Wyoming. Not long afterward, trouble visited Senator Fall.

In April 1922, Fall granted Henry F. Sinclair of the Mammoth Oil Company and Edward L. Doheny of the Pan American Petroleum and Transport Company the rights to drill for oil on Naval Reserves land. Sinclair and Doheny were close friends with Fall, and the senator granted them the rights with no open bidding, contrary to law. After a subsequent congressional investigation of what came to be known as the Teapot Dome Scandal, Fall was found guilty of conspiracy and bribery. According to documents presented to the court, Fall was paid $385,000 by Doheny. It was the first time a Cabinet member was convicted of a felony and sentenced to prison. Fall served nine months of a one-year sentence.

Upon his release from prison, Fall returned to his home in the Tularosa Basin. Not long afterward, Doheny's corporation foreclosed on Fall's property as a result of unpaid loans. Albert Fall died on November 30, 1944, in El Paso, Texas, following a long illness.

CARL ADAMSON

Within weeks following the assassination of Pat Garrett, Carl Adamson, who was at the scene, was placed under arrest for "conspiracy to smuggle Chinese into the United States." He was convicted and sentenced to eighteen months in prison. When he was released, Adamson found employment with a New Mexico sheep rancher whose name was, ironically, Garrett, though he was not related to the late former lawman. Adamson died on November 1, 1919, in Roswell. He was fifty-two years of age.

KILLIN' JIM MILLER

James Brown Miller, best known as Killin' Jim, was also called "Deacon Jim" because of his reported avoidance of alcohol and tobacco and his habit of attending church every Sunday. A paid assassin, writers have attributed at least forty kills to Miller. This is likely an exaggeration, as extant evidence can only verify twelve.

During his lifetime, Miller was employed as a Texas Ranger, a deputy sheriff, a town marshal, a professional gambler, and a professional assassin. In 1909, a year after Pat Garrett was assassinated, Miller was contacted by two men who wished to employ him to kill an Oklahoma cattleman and former US deputy marshal named Gus Bobbit. The men had a personal grudge against Bobbit, and evidence suggested they wanted to take over his ranch.

Using a shotgun, his favored weapon for his work, Miller mortally wounded Bobbit on February 27, 1909, near Ada, Oklahoma. Before he died, Bobbit named Miller as the shooter. Following the assassination, Miller fled to Texas, but was arrested a short time later and returned to Oklahoma to stand trial for murder.

On the morning of April 19, a mob of thirty to forty men stormed the Ada jail and removed Miller along with others believed to be involved with the killing. The prisoners were dragged to an abandoned livery stable behind the jail and hanged from the rafters. Miller was placed on a box while a noose was fastened around his neck. Before he could be pushed from the box, Miller allegedly shouted, "Let 'er rip!" and jumped.

While the death of Killin' Jim Miller has been attributed to an angry mob bent on vengeance and carrying out their own method of justice, recent investigations into the killing of Pat Garrett have revealed the possibility that there was a plan to eliminate Miller, one that may have been orchestrated by W. W. Cox and his companions. It is believed that certain men were concerned that, under questioning, Miller might reveal details of the plot to assassinate Pat Garrett. Three-and-a-half months earlier, Mannen Clements, another member of the Oliver Lee–W. W. Cox band of conspirators, was assassinated in El Paso. The alleged shooter, a man named Joe Brown, was tried but no evidence of his involvement was present and he was found not guilty. Clements had earlier suggested to Albert B. Fall that if certain favors were not granted that he would reveal the names of those involved in the killing of Pat Garrett. It was learned in 2012 that Oliver Lee and W. W. Cox had grown concerned that Clements possessed a great deal of inside information relative to the assassination of Pat Garrett, that he could not be trusted to keep said information to himself, and that he needed to be eliminated. The assassin sent by Oliver Lee to do the job was none other than the dependable Todd Bailey.

WILLIAM WEBB COX

William Webb Cox continued to operate his vast ranch in south-central New Mexico, adding to his holdings over the years by grabbing possession of homesteads, railroad lands, and simply moving into any adjacent area of unsettled property and taking it over. His ranch eventually exceeded one hundred fifty thousand acres, well over 230 sections of land, on which he ran thousands of head of cattle and a herd of one hundred horses, mostly broodmares. In 1910, Cox and his family moved to Las Cruces so his children could attend New Mexico A & M College (now New Mexico State University). Cox died in 1923. He never spoke of his role in the Garrett killing.

During the 1950s, most of the Cox Ranch was acquired by condemnation by the US government for use as part of White Sands Missile Range.

WAYNE BRAZEL

The fate of Wayne Brazel remains one of the biggest mysteries of the Old West. To this day, it is not known what became of him. Following his trial in the killing of Pat Garrett, Brazel came into possession of Harrington Well, located several miles west of Lordsburg in southwestern New Mexico and near the Arizona border. Brazel filed to homestead on 160 acres surrounding the well and moved onto the land with Olive Boyd, who was either his fiancée or his wife; the historical record is unclear on which.

In 1911, Olive gave birth to a son. Her pregnancy had been difficult, and for six months she fought to recover her health. She gradually grew worse and finally succumbed to pneumonia. Brazel, the widowed father of a six-month-old child, was devastated by the loss of his wife and, according to what scant information is available, never got over it.

Brazel sold his Harrington Well property in 1913. Not long afterward, charges of perjury were filed against him by the federal government related to a previous homestead claim. For reasons unclear, the charges were dropped in 1914. A few weeks later, Brazel made arrangements for the care of his son, and then vanished. He left no word with friends or relatives regarding his plans or destination, and to this day no one knows what happened to him. Reports filtered in over the years that Brazel had died a natural death; other reports mentioned that he had been killed.

The reported locations of his demise numbered over a dozen, all scattered across New Mexico and Arizona. None were ever substantiated.

In his book, *The Strange Story of Wayne Brazel*, author Robert Mullin reported that Brazel's son employed El Paso attorney H. L. McCune to investigate his father's disappearance and attempt to learn what happened to him. McCune concluded that the "probable explanation" was that Wayne Brazel journeyed to South America to seek ranching opportunities and was subsequently killed by the "Butch Cassidy gang."

Attorney McCune no doubt collected a fee for his alleged investigative work and the final report, but provided little to nothing in the way of substantiating his findings. Further, prevailing evidence shows that while in South America, Butch Cassidy led no such gang, partnering only with his friend Harry Longabaugh, better known as the Sundance Kid. In truth nothing was ever heard from or about Butch Cassidy after November 7, 1908, a bit over eight months following the killing of Pat Garrett and approximately six years before Wayne Brazel disappeared. To this day, no verifiable information on the fate of Wayne Brazel has ever been located.

TODD BAILEY

Todd Bailey remained with Oliver Lee for only a few weeks after the killing of Pat Garrett. Lee sent him to Haynesville, Louisiana, a small town near the Arkansas border. There, Bailey was to meet with one of Pat Garrett's brothers. The reason for the meeting was never documented, but Bailey family lore claims it had to do with determining whether or not there would be any hostile reaction from the Garrett family relative to the assassination. A short time before Garrett was killed, he was having cattle shipped to New Mexico from Louisiana and Arkansas by his brother. The brother told Bailey there would be no response to the killing of Garrett.

While in Louisiana, Bailey went to a dance across the Arkansas border in the tiny community of Ravanna, where he met his future wife. Bailey returned to New Mexico long enough to take another assignment from Oliver Lee—travel to El Paso, Texas, and kill Mannen Clements. Clements had threatened to expose Lee, Albert B. Fall, W. W. Cox, and several others in the plot to kill Garrett. After carrying out the assignment, Bailey returned to Louisiana. He married on April 12, 1909.

On April 19, Bailey was back in New Mexico during the trial of Wayne Brazel. Oliver Lee was concerned that Carl Adamson, who had been in jail for smuggling illegal Chinese laborers, would arrive to testify and feared that his former accomplice could not be trusted to stand up under intense interrogation in the witness chair. Bailey had orders to shoot and kill Adamson on the road into Hillsboro, New Mexico, where the trial was being held. Adamson, however, declined to testify and never made the trip.

After Brazel's trial, Bailey returned to Louisiana. Shortly thereafter, he and his wife moved to Doddridge, Arkansas, a short distance from Ravanna. Though firmly settled into ranching and other pursuits in southwestern Arkansas, Bailey, according to family history, was summoned from time to time to New Mexico by Oliver Lee to, as it was stated, "take care of business."

With the passage of a few years, southwestern Arkansas was hit hard by the Great Depression, forcing Bailey and his family to move to Broken Bow, Oklahoma, where he raised cattle, operated a butcher shop, and made and sold illegal whiskey. Todd Bailey passed away on August 3, 1949, in Broken Bow.

APPENDIX: DISCOVERING TODD BAILEY

For well over a century, Todd Bailey resided in the nooks and crannies of published history. Those who wrote for what passed for New Mexico history, the life of Pat Garrett, the disappearance of Colonel Albert Jennings Fountain, and the life and times of rancher and politician Oliver Lee chose, for reasons known only to them to ignore this quiet, competent, yet dangerous figure. He was there all the time; they just missed him.

Todd Bailey first came to my attention on November 11, 2011, as I was deep into research on the life and times of Pat Garrett and Oliver Lee. I received an email from a man named Buck Bailey, who was living in Wickes, Arkansas. Mr. Bailey had spotted me on a History Channel program wherein Pat Garrett and Billy the Kid were discussed. Bailey mentioned his grandfather, Todd Bailey, and his connection to Oliver Lee. Mr. Bailey's long email contained a lot of observations on the history and events of New Mexico during the late 1800s and early 1900s, all related to him by his grandfather, Todd Bailey. I was impressed by this provocative load of information, by Bailey's deep insight into people, places, and events. This resulted in several telephone conversations with Buck Bailey wherein we discussed these subjects in depth. During one such conversation, Mr. Bailey said, in passing and as kind of an afterthought, "After my grandfather shot and killed Pat Garrett. . . ."

This stunning comment, one that is antithetical and foreign to every published account of Garrett's assassination, caused me to shout into the phone, "Wait!" I asked Mr. Bailey to back up for a moment and return to his comment about his grandfather killing Garrett. He went into great detail about how and where it had taken place, detail so precise and convincing that it staggered me. I made arrangements for more email and telephone conversations.

Over the next few weeks, I learned more about Todd Bailey's role in the assassination of Pat Garrett, his participation in the killing of Albert J. Fountain and his son, his role in the trial of Oliver Lee, and much more. A great deal of what Buck Bailey told me squared with the history and documentation in my possession, but I needed more verification, substantiation. It was necessary to check out every word spoken by Buck Bailey. I knew just the man to call.

Former federal investigator and now private detective specializing in mysteries of the Old West, Steve Sederwall of Capitan, New Mexico, was at the time working on the Albert Jennings Fountain case and was uncovering heretofore undiscovered documents and evidence. As Buck Bailey was a retired lawman himself, I knew he and Sederwall would get along; they spoke the same cop language and had similar experiences. I put Sederwall in contact with Bailey and asked him to see what he could find out and verify.

What followed was a series of communications between Sederwall and Bailey in which a wealth of pertinent information and insight into the killing of Pat Garrett and the disappearance and killing of the Fountains was revealed.

As an old man, Todd Bailey, living out his final years in southwestern Arkansas, related numerous aspects of his past to his children and grandchildren. Thus was revealed his role in the killing of Pat Garrett, Colonel Fountain, and others. Todd Bailey's past was handed down in his family via the oral tradition. The tales were never in the form of boasting, merely a relating of the facts of what occurred. Todd Bailey never sought recognition or fame for his part in the killing of Albert Fountain, Pat Garrett, and others. His recollections were solely for his children and grandchildren, who, in turn, were cautioned never to repeat them to anyone outside the family. The accounts related by Todd Bailey never changed. Buck Bailey and his siblings became reservoirs for the life story of Todd Bailey, and it was this knowledge he shared with Sederwall and me.

So intrigued was investigator Sederwall with this font of valuable information that in March 2013 he made a trip from his New Mexico home to interview Buck Bailey in person. In addition to Buck, Sederwall interviewed Mike Bailey, a cousin. Buck and Mike had not seen each other in thirty-five years, but they came together to meet with Sederwall to reveal a long and closely guarded family secret. Sederwall and I were the first people outside the family circle to hear the stories of Todd Bailey, stories that came down through two different branches of the family, stories that Buck and Mike shared for the first time in their lives. Their stories were identical in substance.

The day after interviewing Buck and Mike, Sederwall traveled to Oklahoma to interview Buck Bailey's sister, Brenda, who provided more insight and information pertaining to Todd Bailey. Her versions of events were remarkably similar to those of Buck and Mike, and even more detailed.

There was more work ahead for us. Though the Bailey family stories were remarkable in their revelations, it would have been foolhardy to accept them at face value. We now got busy working at validating and verifying everything that was said. If none of the information passed along to us held up under investigation, then we would have wasted a lot of time. As it turned out, we found the versions provided by the members of the Bailey family to be extraordinarily accurate, with details unknown to the so-called historical experts.

During his description of the assassination of Pat Garrett, Buck Bailey included details of the geography of the site that proved to be remarkably precise. Outside of Todd Bailey, neither Buck nor any of his family members had ever been to the site, one that is difficult to reach. Sederwall and I decided to travel to the scene of the killing to examine it in detail. It turned out that Buck Bailey's description of the old road traveled by Garrett just before his death, the nearby ridge, the arroyo, the field of fire, and other aspects were accurate down to the inch. The visit to the site involved a complete walk-through of Buck Bailey's descriptions. The geography was exact; the logistics related to the ambush were on the mark. Even the subsequent mathematical calculation relative to the angle the second bullet entered the body of Garrett and traveled through his body pinpointed Todd Bailey's position in the arroyo 130 feet away.

Buck Bailey is a retired lawman with thirty-seven years of experience. Bailey knows the truth when he sees it. If there was any hokum associated with the stories Todd Bailey told his relatives, Buck would have known it. Bailey is as credible a witness as one could find. Likewise, Sederwall is a skilled interrogator experienced at getting to the truth. By the time Sederwall and I finished dissecting and investigating Buck Bailey's versions of what occurred, we found him to have more credibility than Pat Garrett.

There is more. Recent interviews with Oliver Lee descendants have revealed that they were all aware of Todd Bailey and of his roles in the slaying of Colonel Albert Jennings Fountain, Pat Garrett, and others.

ACKNOWLEDGMENTS

A HUGE DEBT OF GRATITUDE IS OWED THE LATE CHARLES Leland Sonnichsen, who researched and wrote about pertinent historical southern New Mexico goings-on. His books have served as an inspiration for the many who followed in his footsteps.

Steve Sederwall is a veteran law enforcement officer and now a private detective specializing in Old West cold cases. His investigations have turned up heretofore unknown or overlooked documents and information that have contributed much to this book.

Buck Bailey, grandson of Todd Bailey, the assassin of Pat Garrett, gave freely of his time and related some stunning family history held secret for more than a century.

Editor Erin Turner is to be thanked, and praised, for her skills as well as her patience in working with me. As a result of her attention to my manuscripts, I continue to learn more with every submission.

Sandra Bond, agent extraordinaire, has always been helpful, easy to work with, and fun to have lunch and hang out with.

Poet, memoirist, and novelist Laurie Jameson and sometime editor for best-selling authors is always my first reader. Attending to all of the red markings she inflicts on my manuscript always yields a much cleaner and smoother product and makes life a bit easier for my editors.

Illustrator Richard "Peewee" Kolb has worked with me on several books. His images add a great deal to the "feel" of each book, and it is a pleasure to work with him.

SELECTED REFERENCES

BOOKS

Brothers, Mary Hudson. *A Pecos Frontier*. Albuquerque: University of New Mexico Press, 1943.

Curry, George. *An Autobiography*. Albuquerque: University of New Mexico Press, 1958.

Dykes, J. C. *Billy the Kid: Biography of a Legend*. Albuquerque: University of New Mexico Press, 1952.

Etulain, Richard W., and Glenda Riley. *With Badges and Bullets: Lawmen and Outlaws in the Old West*. Golden, CO: Fulcrum, 1999.

Fall, Albert B. *The Memoirs of Albert B. Fall*. Edited by David B. Stratton. Southwestern Studies Series, Vol. IV, No. 3, Monograph No. 15. El Paso: Texas Western Press, 1966.

Garrett, Pat F. *The Authentic Life of Billy, the Kid, the Noted Desperado of the Southwest, Whose Deeds of Daring and Blood Have Made His Name a Terror in New Mexico, Arizona, and Northern Mexico, by Pat Garrett, Sheriff of Lincoln County, N. Mex. By Whom He Was Finally Hunted Down and Captured by Killing Him*. Santa Fe: New Mexico Print and Pub. Co., 1892.

Gibson, A. M. *The Life and Death of Colonel Albert Jennings Fountain*. Norman: University of Oklahoma Press, 1965.

Glenn, Skelton. *Pat Garrett As I Knew Him on the Buffalo Ranges*. Robert N. Mullin Collection, Midland, TX: Haley Memorial Library and History Center, nd.

Horn, Calvin. *New Mexico's Troubled Years*. Albuquerque, NM: Horn and Wallace, 1963.

Hough, Emerson. *The Story of the Outlaw*. New York: Outing Publishers, 1907.

Hutchinson, W. H. *Another Verdict for Oliver Lee*. Clarendon, TX: Clarendon Press, 1965.

———. *A Bar Cross Man: The Life and Personal Writings of Eugene Manlove Rhodes*. Norman: University of Oklahoma Press, 1956.

Hutchinson, W. H., and Robert N. Mullin. *Whiskey Jim and a Kid Named Billie*. Clarendon, TX: Clarendon Press, 1967.

Jameson, W. C. *Billy the Kid: Beyond the Grave*. Lanham, MD: Taylor Trade Publishing, 2005.

———. *Billy the Kid: Investigating History's Mysteries*. Guilford, CT: TwoDot, 2018.

———. *Pat Garrett: The Man Behind the Badge*. Lanham, MD: Taylor Trade Publishing, 2016.

Keleher, William A. *The Fabulous Frontier*. Albuquerque: University of New Mexico Press, 1945.

———. *Violence in Lincoln County*. Albuquerque: University of New Mexico Press, 1957.

McCarty, John L. *Maverick Town: The Story of Old Tascosa*. Norman: University of Oklahoma Press, 1946.

Meadows, John P. (ed. John P. Wilson). *Pat Garrett and Billy the Kid As I Knew Them*. Albuquerque: University of New Mexico Press, 2004.

Metz, Leon C. *Pat Garrett: The Story of a Western Lawman*. Norman: University of Oklahoma Press, 1974.

Mullin, Robert. *The Strange Story of Wayne Brazel*. Canyon, TX: Palo Duro Press, 1969.

Poe, John W. *The Death of Billy the Kid*. Boston: Houghton Mifflin, 1933.

Poe, Sophie A. *Buckboard Days*. Albuquerque: University of New Mexico Press, 1981.

Prassel, Frank Richard. *The Great American Outlaw: A Legacy of Fact and Fiction*. Norman: University of Oklahoma Press, 1993.

Recko, Corey. *Murder on the White Sands*. Denton: University of North Texas Press, 2007.

Richards, Colin. *How Pat Garrett Died*. Santa Fe, NM: Palomino Press, 1970.

Rister, Carol Coke. *Fort Griffin on the Texas Frontier*. Norman: University of Oklahoma Press, 1956.

Scanlon, John Milton. *Life of Pat Garrett*. El Paso, TX: Southwest Printing Company, 1952.

Shinkle, James D. *Reminiscences of Roswell Pioneers*. Roswell, NM: Hall-Poorbaugh Press, 1966

Shirley, Glen. *Shotgun for Hire: The Story of "Deacon" Jim Miller, the Killer of Pat Garrett*. Norman: University of Oklahoma Press, 1970.

Sonnichsen, C. L. *Tularosa: Last of the Frontier West*. Albuquerque: University of New Mexico Press, 1960.

Sonnichsen, C. L., and William V. Morrison. *Alias Billy the Kid*. Albuquerque: University of New Mexico Press, 1955.

Tatum, Stephen. *Inventing Billy the Kid*. Albuquerque: University of New Mexico Press, 1982.

Tuska, Jon. *Billy the Kid: A Handbook*. Lincoln: University of Nebraska Press, 1989.

Utley, Robert M. *Billy the Kid: A Short and Violent Life*. Lincoln: University of Nebraska Press, 1989.

REPORT

Investigative Report in the Disappearance of Albert Jennings Fountain and Henry Fountain, March 6, 1896–May 13, 1896. Pinkerton's National Detective Agency. Chicago, Illinois.

INTERVIEWS

Numerous interviews with Buck Bailey, Wickes, Arkansas, from November 2011 through 2016.

INDEX

ABOUT THE AUTHOR

W. C. Jameson is the award-wining author of more than one hundred books, over a thousand articles, and has appeared on numerous television documentaries and historical series. He lives in Texas.